INVESTED OR RAT RACE TRAPPED?

INVESTED OR RAT RACE TRAPPED?

EASY STEPS TO BREAKFREE

Authored by

Ashish Bhave | Rashmi Bhamare | Rikita Shah

Penman Books

Office No. 303, Kumar House Building,
D Block, Central Market, Opp PVR Cinema,
Prashant Vihar, Delhi 110085, India
Website: www.penmanbooks.com
Email: publish@penmanbooks.com

First Published by Penman Books 2019
Copyright © Ashish Bhave | Rashmi Bhamare | Rikita Shah 2019
All Rights Reserved.

Title: Invested or Rat Race Trapped?
Price: ₹550 | $14
ISBN: 978-93-89024-45-6

Acknowledgement

From Ashish Bhave

"I am really thankful to all my clients and participants of my investor awareness program.

These are people who actually helped me to understand what is a real practical relevance of my information about financial management. They are helping me to convert information to knowledge.

They ask questions and I have to think for a practical relevant solutions, this process enriched my knowledge.

I am thankful to my colleagues and fraternity to enrich my knowledge which I can put in this book.

I am thankful to my Father - **Ramesh Bhave**, Mother - **Ragini Bhave**, wife - **Aparna**, daughter - **Madhura** and sister - **Shamika Dixit** who supported me in my every decision.

I am thankful to my guide and friend **Sanjeev Ogale, Vidyadhar Katkar, Milind Bhamare, Bharatbhushan Kolhe** who had trusted me since beginning of my career.

I am thankful to **GOD** - Energy of universe who had given me this opportunity to serve investor through this book.

I am thankful to **Rashmi Bhamare** and **Rikita Shah** for their contribution as co-author of this book.

The list is really big because I got lot of help from many and still getting.

At last I am thankful to everyone with gratitude who touched my life positively, inspired me, motivated me.

I wish Rich and Happy life to everyone."

From Rashmi Bhamare

"Writing the book is harder than I thought and more rewarding and satisfying than I could have ever imagined. None of this would have been possible without my better half **Milind Bhamare**. He stood by me like a true friend, during every struggle and all my successes. He was there to read the early "shit" draft and to make it look like a book. He is as important to this book getting done as I was.

My sincere thanks to co-author **Ashish Bhave** for his encouragement, guidance, knowledge, experience but mostly for his simplicity, his best wishes for my success and his deep concern about financial wellbeing for everyone. Thanks a lot for gifting me your precious time to mentor me. Tonnes of thank you to my second co-author **Rikita Shah**. Thanks to your knowledge, great interest in reading books, your creativity and effectively managing the work. Your habit of going out of the way has helped us a lot to shape up this book. Your dedicated efforts has made the book more interesting and trendy. I truly enjoy being a part of this team.

Many of my friends have helped me to arrange Investor's awareness camps in their companies, organizations, societies and groups. Like **Anand Deshpande, Vivek Takawale, Rajendra Mulay** and many more.

I am thankful to my friend and well-wisher **Parag Kale, Padma Apte, Rahul Bhamare, Dipali Kesaria** and many more who had trusted me since beginning of my career.

Thanks a million,

To my family,

To Aai-Pappa **(Mrs Indira & Mr Ashok Bhamare)** who also write articles in the Sr. Citizen's Magazine has motivated me to write.

To Aai, Baba **(Mrs Suruchi & Mr Surendra Aghor)** for being there to turn to during those dark and desperate times.

To brother **Ketan**, I have never felt the need to ask for your help, because you have always been there before I even had to ask. Thanks bro.

To Bhavjay **Tanmayee** for your understanding and reaching out.

To my daughters **Sayali & Mitali** to understand my time constraint while writing this book and also taking care of yourself when I was not around.

Thank you ..!! from the bottom of my heart to each individual and households who have enriched me to become a person that I am today."

From Rikita Shah

"I would like to thank my family. Mother, **Bhavna Shah,** father **Kirti Shah,** and brother **Harshil Shah**.

Family being the immediate surrounding is always the one to be given the immediate credit to, because it is for them that I had the ability to be able to dream in the first place.

My father's protection, mother's love, and brother's honest critique have allowed me to have the wings to realize the dream.

My uncles **Bhupendra Shah** and **Jaysukh Shah**, helped me see all the hurdles that may come on my path and made me ready to face them by providing their insight and sharing their experiences.

Manan Shah, my Fiancé (by the time you read this book, he shall have become my Husband), he made my dream - his dream, helped me to set my priorities straight, and always helped me stay focused and motivated. His support added strength to my wings.

Parents- in law- **Amul Shah** and **Neeta Shah**, Sisters in Law – **Shrushti Shah** and **Natasha Shah** for their support enabled me to spread my wings wider so that I can fly higher.

To all my friends and colleagues for giving me the jump, being a constant source of support, energy and a head start whenever I venture into the unknown, special thanks to **Aarya Jadhav** for being a great helping hand, providing a different perceptive and for being practically my task manager, **Ashish Bhave** and **Rashmi Bhamre** for being such great co-authors, co-operative and supportive and making sure we flew in the same direction.

From all the co-authors of this book:

Reading or thinking about writing a book is easy, but actually, it is as arduous as it gets. One always needs to be pulled, pushed or goaded on and we were lucky to find some extraordinary support that helped us make it this far."

Our Publishing House - **Penman Books** who always made it a point to keep us on track, our publishing manager Tarun Singh, Cover designer Neeraj Sharma and rest of the team have played a crucial role by being ahead and guiding us, these people marked by generosity, have always gone an extra mile to make ends meet.

Our Graphic Designer **Sourabh Ingale** (Instagram Handle- Sourabh_Ingale2705), adept in his art, has been able to seamlessly transform our thoughts into images that come alive as you come across them further on in the book.

Milind Bhamare for being the extra hand that we need, his support and knowledge marked a crucial role throughout our journey.

Sachin Pawar, Owner of Shree Arts (Instagram Handle- sachin.letters), whose novel perception and flawless execution helped us to design and develop our "Financial Freedom Game"

Manan Shah, Founder of The Other side Photography (Instagram handle - theothersidephotography) who was able to fit inside a still frame, our dream and our story.

And our **Readers**, we would like to extend our gratitude towards you as well, without you the book would have not found its purpose, thank you for becoming a part of this book now.

Preface

Most of the financial traps written in this book are really around each one of us and in few of these we were also trapped. These are the experiences of us and of the individuals whom we are meeting.

This book is for everyone who have learned to live with the pain of being in Rat Race Trap or are struggling to be happy by copying others lifestyle which is not helping them.

Ignorance and Financial Illiteracy are the two key reasons for financial hardships for individual and households. After meeting many individual and families and started getting practical problems they are facing, they don't know how much they have, how much they need, how much to spend and where to invest.

This book is intended to reach every such individual who want to know simple, easy, practical but effective way to manage their money. It shall help you burst all the myths that you held forever. The book is written in a simple way that even a person who knows nothing about finance or financial planning will be able to understand and manage their money well. The book shall be great at all milestones of life like started earning, growing earnings and expenses and retirement.

In this book we have listed down the traps and their solutions. You will find the situations which will make you realise severity of trap that you are into or may get into. It will help you to visualise your future lifestyle what you could afford and what not.

Simple solutions depend on first acknowledging the traps that one is into, realizing its severity and then finding the root cause of it. It could be just an ignorance or a thought process or a belief or a habit.

Before this book we have indigenised a Financial Freedom Game. It's a board game to help people understand different scenarios in personal life affecting their own finance. We have conducted Financial Wellbeing camps in corporates, published articles and quotes on financial awareness.

Read this book and let us know your comments.

We are eager to hear from you.

Financial Freedom Game

A game about Earning, Spending, Saving, and Investing

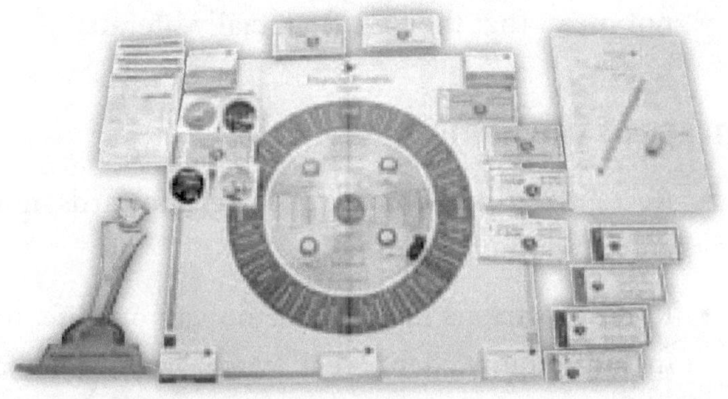

About the Game

- We have designed the Financial Freedom Game (board game). It is the first **indigenised Personal financial board game.**

- It helps to go through different stages of financial Life, giving practical insight into how to take financial decisions in your life.

- Its main purpose is to help participants from all walks of life (including common man, entrepreneurs, corporate professionals, students, educators, homemakers, investors) attain **financial literacy** and becoming **financially strong**.

- Financial Freedom is the dream of most of the individuals, individuals strive for that, they earn and save to reach to financial freedom but unfortunately, it keeps on running away from them.

- The main reason for this is Financial Illiteracy, having a great education and earning well, does not mean that they are financially literate.

Concept of the Game

- Recognize your **behavioral pattern** towards money and investments

- Roles of various investment tools in our life, tools include equity, debt, real estate, cash, gold, and mutual fund as a vehicle And Insurance includes Life, medical, car insurance as a part of the protection system.

- Learn where you need to be, in wealth accumulation or wealth creation phase.

- Understand the key features for creating passive income.

- Educate Participants on achieving financial well-being, help them get started with basic tasks to manage their personal finances better.

- Guide you all towards long-term wealth creation and fulfillment of life's financial goals & dreams.

Why this concept

"I wish they taught us about money in school!"

- Learning about money and *finance* does *not* have to be dull and boring.

- We found that **8 out of 10** cases, investors' personal finance is in a mess.

- They don't know how to decipher monthly statements.

- Lack of Knowledge as to when/where/how to invest.

- In most cases, the spouses (normally the women) are not aware of the financial planning done by their husbands, or fathers.

Our Role

- So we came up with this book as well as a game where one can learn these things on their own

- We want young people and adult learners to take the time to study and master the basics of *financial* concepts but through an innovative way that would capture their attention.

- The good news is that we are making financial literacy **fun.**

- Finance is important, dynamic, interesting, engaging and *enjoyment here.*

The benefit to the player

- Will help players to understand how they can manage their finance while dealing with life scenarios (Related to personal financial management.) they can come across in their life.

- Here you can fast forward time and see your financial future, All this happens in a couple of hours, you could get a chance to check whether your today's money management strategies are taking you to financial freedom?

- If you know your financial future and you are not happy with it, you can change some things to create a new future for you

- Facing such challenges of real-life scenarios in the game, You will be able to take this experience from reel-to-real life.

- The experience might include how & why to invest to generate passive income, avoid or control expenses, and impact of their today's decisions in the future.

- The game covers all such related scenarios plus different types of investment tools available in the market, for them to understand which particular asset class can help them and in what way.

This is all about the "Financial Freedom" game, where you get to experience your future as this game is about your money management strategies.

Every turn you are taking financial decisions that will create your future.

With the enjoyment of mistakes and success, you learn lessons of financial management to achieve a life of freedom.

This game has helped 100+ people to take experience & Successfully implement investment decisions thereafter. Here is what our few participants have felt after playing the game.

'Financial Freedom Game' is a fantastic game that will help tune your mindset towards systematic financial management by setting your short term and long term financial goals and help meet those goals. This game is a beginning towards your systematic financial planning to help you build long term wealth.

—Chetan Doddanavar

This game actually makes you aware of situations that can come to you as a surprise & unexpected in future life. Based on this crafted experience you start thinking unconsciously at events of life which help to plan & make wise decisions in the interest of ourselves & our family.

Great wisdom & actual freedom.

—*Gouri & Santosh Tipale*

Many more feedbacks and reviews are available on our facebook page, and to know about the game or to play the game in the upcoming session you can follow us and get connected to us through facebook (@ FinancialFreedomGame)or   Instagram(Invested_or_rat_race_trapped).

You learn best when your Education is an Experience with Enjoyment

How to Read the Book

The book is been divided into 3 part,

The First Part: Shall explain to you what is Rat Race and how one gets into it, here you need to introspect and check if you too have been through this or if you are going through this currently.

Second Part: Shall show how your few or all strategies till now have made you poor and got up into the trap about which you were unaware till date, make a list of where all you are trapped and need to change the strategies.

Third Part: Shall provide you with simple and easy steps to follow to get out of the trap and start investing with the right strategies.

Quick Financial Plan: At the end of the book you shall find a quick and easy financial planning page, with the help of knowledge you gain by reading the book and this page you shall be able to plan your goals and achieve them in the right way.

Wishing you a Rich and Happy Life

Contents

PART 3
Freedom from Rat Race Trap (RRT)

PART
One

Rat Race Trap

After graduating as a Computer Engineer, it took me almost 10 months to get my first job. I had friends who graduated at the same time and got a job offer in sundry technology companies. This was way back in early 2000. We used to hear them glorifying about their company's campus, training, Job profile, and facilities. I was appearing for sundry tech companies interview striving to commence my professional career. Conclusively, after 10 months of struggle, I got culled in one of the topmost Indian IT companies in Bangalore after 3 rounds of the interview.. The company was a dream company for me and for many youngsters wanting to make a career in IT / Software. IT Sector then was a sunrise industry promising lucrative career, high paid jobs, and onsite opportunities. I was all exhilarated to commence my professional journey. First thing was to tell parents about this good news and make them proud. Now they need not have to send me the money and I can give them a better and luxurious lifestyle.

Since it was the start of a career for me, I wanted to make an impression, create that visibility to my bosses and set my path to success. My days would start early in the morning and I would always work for more than 10 -12 hours a day, sometime even over the weekend. The companies also used to offer a lot of freebies like delicious snacks and beverages in the evening, free bus or cab service for people staying late. The world-class facilities like gym, swimming pool, various recreational facilities, free internet, hobby classes were all there for us to keep motivated to work long and slog.

Then came the memorable day of my first salary. My first pay. I opened my mailbox the Morning after reaching to work. There was this magical email containing the payslip. I was excited to see how much money has been credited to my salary account. And frankly speaking, I was a bit disappointed. The salary credited in the bank was not the same as what was told in the offer letter. I looked at the salary slip and there were few deductions with words like Company Contribution towards PF, Employee Contribution towards PF, Income Tax, and Professional Tax. All of these were bouncers for me. No one in my academic courses had told me about how salaried employees pay structure would look like. My Father was Manager in a reputed PSU bank. He neither told me about the same. Maybe discussing financial matters is not a culture in many households and we were no exception. After taking a second look at the payslip I realized that almost 20% of my pay was deducted as Tax on Income. I was now a bit shocked and a little bit annoyed as well. The term itself looked funny to me. Why someone should be taxed for earning money? I was facing the real world now. Throughout my entire academic career, I was always told that I was being prepared for "the real world." But once I entered the working world in earnest, I soon realized that academic education can never fully prepare you for it.

I was in a reputed company, the company famous for transparency and corporate governance standards. So definitely it will not cheat me. But I still checked with a couple of buddies who had also joined with me. After all, we turn to friends to get advises and validate something which we are not sure of or don't understand, isn't it?

Husshhh... Happy to see that their payslip also carried similar deductions. Yes, it would have been more painful to see friends getting more salary than me. So there is nothing wrong. One of my friends made a classic comment – **'Dude, don't think too much on deductions. Have we ever thought to get such a high pay package at the beginning of our career only! I suddenly realized, my first paycheck was almost equivalent to my dad's then-current pay who was about to retire in another 4-5 years.** So we all settled with an agreement that there is nothing wrong with pay slip and almost a quarter of salary may get deducted as Tax. Albeit, no one still understood the formula and rationale behind tax deduction.

Now it's time to celebrate. It's an achievement and I must pamper myself with shopping and gifts. We all went to a lavish restaurant for dinner. For the first time in my life, it was MY money and I was going to pay for my own dinner. Now I am an independent woman. It's a dream to be independent. I ended up spending almost all money within a fortnight on movies, shopping (for self and near & dear ones), outing, and dinner. Felt empowered. Felt Rich. And then I also realized…oh, there are certain bills that I have yet to pay? Rent, Electricity. And I have spent almost all of my salary. Back to the square? I asked my dad to send me the money for my survival for the remainder of the month until I get the next paycheck to get that zing of empowerment and richness.

A year down the line –I was kind of settled in the job. I was single and by now started getting accustomed to 'work hard, party harder' culture of ITians. Yes, I was proud to be an IT Professional with a bright career ahead and a lot more money in the future.

Money... Oh, money. The more you make, the more they take! And now that since I am an independent, empowered lady, I had slowly learned to handle my money and bank account.

The bank is placed similarly to the temple, where all kind of people walk in and out with all various demands and issues right from morning 9.30 till evening till the gates don't shut for the customers.

Temple is a spiritual place where people ask God to help them with luck and strength to complete their dreams. And in a similar way bank is a place where their dreams are fulfilled (saving account) or they are given wings (loans).

Once I had to visit my bank to carry some financial transactions. Online banking was still in a nascent stage during early 2000. I was waiting for my turn to come.

Since I did not have any other thing to do (there were no WhatsApp, FB, Instagram. In fact there were no smartphones. Mobile industry was in the early evolution phase), I started observing people around me. There was a queue for ATM, a separate line for cheque holders, another related to loans and so on. There were life insurance agents, credit card agents pitching hard to people to purchase their products. Everyone seemed to be busy.

There was an uncle sitting next to me, waiting for his passbook to get updated. He started talking to me. After an initial formal greeting, the conversation got to the financials. He advised me to get the passbook regularly updated. Keep the track of expenses and find out if I am making some unnecessary or stupid expenses (which surely I was). If you don't do this then you will be in a trap, he continued.

Trap? What Trap? I asked him. Rat Race Trap, he said. The trap which you build on your own to financially ruin yourself at the end like the spider. We were puzzled. We had never heard anything like this before. His words were not making sense to me. "Sorry Sir, I don't understand what you are saying", we exclaimed!

He smiled and started sharing his knowledge with me. And his story started with the same typical old way.

"When I was 25, I started my job in an engineering firm. My salary was ₹10,000. This was around 35 years back, the old man said. There were fewer engineers and ₹10,000 was considered to be a huge amount. As soon as I got my 1st salary, I knew exactly what to do with it. I went to the temple, put some money there in the donation box, then went straight to the market, brought gifts & sweets for all family members. I had money in my pocket so I hired an auto instead of traveling by bus. Slowly my standard of living started getting higher and so the expenses. But I was ok with it since my salary was also growing. I also started putting some money aside as my savings. What I did not realize was that the rate at which my salary and savings were growing were far lesser than my expenses. And then my family got bigger. Wife, children and parents, and then it made my expenses run at full speed.

Initially, I used to work hard because I used to like it. Then I worked harder because I started liking money more than work. The money helped me buy happiness for myself and my loved ones. But the problem with money and happiness is it keeps on coming and going. **To buy more happiness more money was needed and so more and more hard work was required.** And this cycle kept on going month after month, year after year. This is what I call it a Rat Race Trap. I could not come out of it. Now I am retired and now living on my retirement fund (Pension, Gratuity). Now I need to keep track of all expenses since I have limited money and I should not come to a situation where I am left with zero money to take care of my sunset years."

Our conversation was interrupted when a bank employee came in to hand over the updated passbook to him. He left waving me goodbye. But surely I was handed over a big lesson of my life. I thought I need to do something different to stay away from the trap. But how? Who would guide me?

Fast Forward - I was almost five years in the job now. And I had started realizing that with every promotion and salary increment the income tax was eating bigger pie. The more you earn, the more you will pay tax. Initially, I used to pay 20% of my pay in tax. Now it was in the range of 30%. Then with every budget, the government will announce some welfare scheme, to provide for it, will add a surcharge or cess on already highly taxed income. I also realized that shopping malls, restaurants are one step ahead of you. You may get an increment of 5% per year but the cost of goods, materials, and food used to be up by 8-10%. All of a sudden the sandals /shoes that used to cost Rs 300 to 500 were no more for me. I am an IT professional and I must now switch to branded shoes / clothes /perfumes.

Finally, I deserve to be get pampered with the money that I am earning. Someone told me that this is called inflation, **lifestyle inflation**. The net result was, the more we earn, the more we spent and at the end of the month like any salaried individual my bank account would go dry. I felt that the more I earn the more I am becoming poor? Somewhere I had read that for wealthy people despite spending lavishly, their bank account never goes dry.

Meanwhile, I got married and Income got double. We both were from high paying IT sector; we thought we have firmly set ourselves on the path to become RICH and to live a wealthy life.

However, somewhere the calculations were going erroneous. Something was certainly not right. Despite having the double income I commenced realizing that we are not able to keep much. We were struggling to ascertain what was taking a toll on our dream lifestyle. The pattern of feeling like a poor till the terminus of the month perpetuated. Amid this confusion, one of my friends reintroduced a concept of 'Rat Race Trap'. It immediately made me recall the conversation with that old wise man in the bank. Rat Race Trap - **An endless, self-defeating or pointless pursuit.** Just like rats attempting to earn a reward like cheese, to no avail.

This is a story of one of our Author.

In a simple term, Rat Race Trap **can be defined as a way of life in which people are caught up in a fiercely competitive struggle for wealth or power resulting in a repetitive lifestyle that leaves no time for relaxation or enjoyment. It becomes an endless struggle.**

The people in the Rat Race Trap are always running, always in some kind of financial problems or financial insecurity. The scary part is they are fiercely competing without knowing where they want to go? It is like a ship in the ocean without a compass not knowing which direction it is heading and where the destination is?

CHAPTER
One

What is Rat Race Trap?

Rat Race is a condition of your life, where your finances bring TRP in Life. Now, what is TRP in life? It's Tension, Restlessness, and Panic as a part of your life.

You have tension about and around money. You are not feeling secure about your financial future. You are running away from financial situations, from financial responsibilities. You are running in search of happiness. As you are living in a materialistic world, you think that spending money on luxuries will buy you and your family happiness. And to keep up to the expenses most of the time you are running for money. Most of the time you are in some kind of financial problem or you are afraid that your lifestyle may land in a problem in the near future.

Financial problems love you; want to stay with you. You try and find out some solution but unfortunately, you end up having a new problem.

Your every solution comes with a new problem. It is like a problem coming in the gift wrap of solutions. Surprisingly this happens again and again. No matter how fast or how slow you run, you find yourself standstill.

And after a few days of your efforts, you start accepting that problems are part and parcel of life and there is no way out (this is worst). These financial problems squeeze you, depress you and completely drain you out. Your dreams disappear. You work because you want money with the hope that someday some miracle will take away your financial problems.

Points to Ponder

- There is a need to increase your awareness about finances to protect yourself from Rat Race Trap.

- If you don't take care of your finances you will automatically fall into the Rat Race Trap.

- Running in a Rat Race Trap is a race without a destination.

- If you are struggling to meet up your expenses then there is a great possibility that you are already in a Rat Race Trap.

CHAPTER
Two

Trap? What is that?

"Those who speak of progression but afraid to change ourself-repressed and therefore unable to reach any further than their eyes can already see."

—Criss Jami

Not having a foresight, one of the reasons for getting trapped? Having limited beliefs is getting trapped? Or it's our greed that gets us in here? Or the eagerness to keep on doing old things with the new situation getting us trapped? Or half knowledge about that particular thing?

Let's first define what a trap is!

- The trap is a situation where you get in, but do not know how to come out. In the process of coming out, you get more trapped inside, and then give up the hope of finding a way out.

- It is what happens with the Rat too. When he is in a cage, he runs on the treadmill, thinking he might reach somewhere. And when he realizes he is not reaching anywhere, he still continues to do the same because he has nothing else to do. When he is running on the treadmill and you open the cage to let him out, he will see that the door is open but will still continue running on the treadmill… Why so!!! Maybe he is now used to run on that and believes he will reach somewhere rather than running out of the cage.

This is what happens with us too, our treadmill starts on the day when we start earning money. At the beginning of the income generation process, people have an idea and a mind that, if I have more money in my wallet, I will really enjoy my life. I will be happy.

So people work for money and in pursuit of happiness, they reach a destination called buying.

Buying gives happiness and it brings facilities, comfort, lifestyle. But unfortunately, that happiness is short-lived. One starts craving more. And as a result, money starts disappearing. You need more money and then you keep working even harder. This ultimately lands you in an unhappy situation called– TRP (Tension, restlessness, and panic).

Work for Money (In hope that it will bring happiness) → **Spend to get happiness** (Short-lived happiness) → **Money crunch** (No Money, No Buying happiness) → **Unhappy** → Need more money to spend (Solution) → (Way out) **go to work**, work harder till body permits and then start compromising life.

This is a trap.

Points to Ponder

- Whether buying material things (shopping) is giving you long term Trappiness?
- Beware whatever is attracting you, maybe taking you into a trap.
- Is your graph of happiness too volatile?

CHAPTER
Three

Rat Race Trap Symptoms

Like any other disorder, Rat Race Trap is a financial Disorder. Any health disorder can be identified by its indications which are called Symptoms. You check the symptoms and know what the health issue could be. But is that possible with your financial health too? Does Rat Race Trap have common Symptoms too?

Yes, it has! Like all other disorders, it also has some peculiar indications.

Check the below list, If you are going through any of these situations then you are already in Rat Race Trap (RRT)

I. Most of the times you are under financial stress

The financial problem is behind you, financial situations are troubling you. It comes in the form of EMI, Unplanned & Impulsive Expenses, School fees, Vehicle breakdown, Unexpected expenses, like some kind of emergencies and so on.

You are Constantly borrowing from someone, compromising even on your basic and mandatory financial needs. Your credit card outstandings have swollen to a level much higher than your monthly earnings. You always feel a financial crunch towards the end of the month or keep postponing paying your monthly bills. If you experience a similar kind of symptoms then there is a great possibility that you are stressed every month. Every month comes with a challenge to meet the ends. This can happen irrespective of your earnings.

II. Fear of Financial future:

Ask yourself, am I facing a financially stressed situation? How does my financial future look like? Am I constantly worrying about the financial future? If there are some temporary setbacks like job loss, do I have enough cushion to maintain all my financial commitments for at least a year?

III. Your happiness lasts small:

When you are happy, you are still worried about your financial future and when you are stressed you are dreaming of happiness. The happiness derived out of the financial indulgence spa is short-lived, perishable. You forget TRP for a while. But at the roots, there are worries about the future, worries about commitments, and worries about meeting up financial requirements.

IV. Money controls you

You are in the mid-forties or above and are getting a feeling that you had worked for many years, you earned handsome, had not spent much but still do not have enough with you! You feel that you are messed up with income and expenses. You are in a situation where you do not have control over your money but money controls you.

V. Solution or New Problem?

You discuss your financial problems with the people around you to get some advice. But unfortunately, every solution comes with a new problem. If these are the basic solution you get as advice, you apply

- Earning more money by weekend working or overtime
- Changing the company
- Taking a loan
- Using credit card
- Investing in the risky asset to get high returns

Then after a few attempts, you understand that efforts are futile and you find yourself often to ground zero.

Every attempt to get a solution to TRP takes you to the wrong path. Unfortunately, most people accept it as a fact of life. They feel that you can't have a life without financial problems. But it's not true, your life can be very smooth financially if you take the right steps and adopt the right solutions.

There are few people who accept the problem as a part of life, there are few who adopt this from Childhood as they have been trained by parents. Whatever may be the reason the result is RRT.

Getting out of RRT is not about winning the Race. It's about getting exit from this Race. That's the real freedom from the RRT.

Points to Ponder

- Think about these 5 points given below. If you think it's happening with you then you are in the already in RRT.
- Most of the times you are under financial stress
- Fear of Financial future
- Your happiness lasts small, a short period of time
- Money controls you
- Solution or New Problem?

CHAPTER
Four

Who Are in Rat Race Trap?

There are four ways to earn money:

Work for someone

- Where you will get a fixed income (Salary) every month.

Self Employed

- You are in some profession, working as an individual.

Business Owners

- You employ people and they work for you and you pay them fixed income.

Investors

- You make investments in income-earning opportunities.

Most of the people believe that financially successful people are from the 3rd or 4th category. But it's not true entirely. Even Self-employed and salaried people also can get Financial Freedom.

As per the recent 2018 report by Oxfam top 9 billionaires in India own as much as half of the country. As per the Wikipedia report, the richest 1% of Indians own 58.4% of the wealth. The richest 10 % of the Indians own 80.7 % of the wealth. These are the people who are either business owners or investors and they are controlling maximum wealth.

People who fall under the category of Salary or Self Employed are stuck in the rat race trap and they are just going round and round with virtually no escape. Every morning they have to go for work so that they can pay their bills and support the lifestyle they desire. They work hard so that they can stay ahead of the competition and can get more money, more promotion, and more increments. Sometimes they do this by making sacrifices at a personal level. There may be a school function where their kid is participating, they may want to attend that family event/ gathering where there is a chance to meet all near and dear ones after a long time. But they skip (most of the time forcefully) those personal commitments so that they don't miss the deadlines that their employer has set for them. Despite this, they are under a constant threat of job security. No one knows when an employer may find an employee irrelevant and can terminate their jobs. These people despite earning handsome money are not aware of how much they need for their comfortable retirement. Are they financially secured? In case of an unfortunate event of job loss how long they can financially survive? They don't know these answers. They don't have time. So what best they can do is to go to a job every morning even when they are not happy.

In the social gatherings these people will vent out their frustration on how bad their company is, how despite being working hard they are underpaid or are not getting good increments or promotions, how their boss favors that one particular employee and how fast he or she is climbing the ladder fast, how their work-life balance has gone for toss, so on and so forth. Some of them feel that changing jobs may solve the problem. But few days in the new job and they realize that it is just that name of the company that is changed. The rest of the aspects is the same. Old Wine in New Bottle kind of situation. Rat Race Trap Continues.

The self-employed class is no different. They are sailing in the same boat as a salaried class. The shop owners, lawyers, doctors, etc fall into this category. For them to earn and sustain their lifestyle, their physical presence is absolutely needed. Their earning capacity is directly proportional to their skills. A shop owner neither can leave the shop nor can he keep it shut for more than a day or two in case he needs to attend certain personal or family commitments. Doctor or Lawyer continuously needs to be updated with the latest trend in their profession else they can get outsmarted by new young, dynamic people.

In the case of a businessman, he is directly responsible for everything in the business. They have to pay salaries to their employees even if there is a business or not. Has to face changes in government trading policies, business policies, tax structures, labor laws, and many such changes. He has to take care of his clients, may have to give services or goods on credit with understanding that the client will pay in time and business will continue smooth. But it happens with very few businesses and that so most of the businesses cannot survive more than 3 years.

In the case of Investors, one wrong investment can ruin the entire profits. So while doing investments, an investor has to do a lot of research. They need to be updated with the latest trend in the business environment, socioeconomic changes, government policies, Capital gain changes, micro, and macroeconomics. An investor has to invest at the right time as well as the exit at the right time and the reality is you can't predict the right time.

So it doesn't mean that you have to be a businessman or investor to be free from RRT. You can apply the same strategies which are used by many people who have earned RRT Freedom. We will discuss these strategies in the coming up sections.

There are many reasons why people are in RRT. One of the reasons is, Indian households find it difficult to manage the rising education and health care expenses.

Unfortunately in a country like India, the government managed education and primary healthcare has to come a long way before a common citizen can think of availing them. We have to pay the tax on our earning and also have to make provision for our healthcare, children's education, and their retirement. With expenses in medical and education continually outpacing the earning pattern, coming out of the RRT just becomes a distant dream and people have to run in the trap irrespective of whether they like or not. The vicious cycle continues and people knowingly or unknowingly become part of it.

Points to Ponder

- You can be in an RRT irrespective of your earning style i.e. Salaried, Professional, Businessman or even if an Investor.

- This also means that everyone has an equal opportunity to get Freedom from RRT.

- So change in style of earning may not be the right solution to get Freedom from RRT.

CHAPTER
Five

What Causes Rat Race Trap?

*"We are what our thoughts have made us;
so take care about what you think. Words are secondary.
Thoughts live; they travel far."*

—Swami Vivekananda

In the previous chapter, we talked about the different learning patterns of the people. In this chapter, we will extend this further to spending habits. The spending habits, in fact, are the very cause of Rat Race Trap.

The financial position of the parents, the money culture at home, the surroundings & neighborhood, schooling, etc bears a great impact on the upbringing of an individual. The skills, education, degree, your career choice are more or less dependent upon these factors. Naturally, your attitude towards money also gets shaped as a part of your upbringing. If someone's money habits are not right then having any earning pattern and even inheriting a legacy from past generations may not help them to get Freedom from Rat Race Trap.

In most of the cases, it so happens that an individual is not aware of financial literacy or money management. These are the subjects which are rarely taught in the school. Also, there is very little scope of cognizance of the same in households when many of the parents themselves are financially illiterate. Parents think that kids will know about money management on their own once they start earning which is a very crude thought process. It is strange that in our country we take bigger life decisions without even checking if we are prepared for that. We are in most cases fortuitous husbands, or wives or even parents without knowing what it takes to get into that role.

There is this interesting say – 'एक बार इंसान पानी में गिर जाए तो हाँथ-पैर मारना सीख ही लेता है।' Frankly speaking this saying always sounded funny to us (in fact more of a stupid). How many of you can simply jump in the water without knowing how to swim and without having a coach to start with? Forget about deep water, swimming in 4ft water can prove to be fatal.

So we throw these kids, now grown into adults to face the financial challenges of life without adequately providing them with the right awareness/resources/arms & ammunition. They don't have a proper starter kit and hence they don't know anything about financial planning. And this becomes the first step towards a rat race trap.

The income they start receiving by trading their time and skills gives them a feeling of empowerment. The instant gratification they get by spending that money on luxuries of life makes them happy.

We are not saying that these young professionals should not spend on luxuries. They certainly deserve that pampering. Ultimately it is the reward of their hard work. The problem starts when **this gratification** becomes an **addiction**. Spending lavishly and mindlessly becomes a habit, a culture, a lifestyle. Slowly they start adding more liabilities to their life. They now feel an urge to upgrade their lifestyle. The shoes or clothes from the local vendor do not suit their standard of living. They become more brand conscious. The 2 wheeler no more suits their lifestyle. They need a car. They own multiple credit cards in their wallets. Purchasing an expensive item by using a credit card takes them to the top of the world (That's what they think).

They now meet someone charming whom they want to spend the life with. The rented apartment gets upgraded to owned flat. There are so nice people around in the form of bankers and builders. They will make you feel that the flat that you are going to purchase is the unique of its own kind in the entire world and the loan that banks will give you will be one with the lowest interest rate and maximum benefits.

Life moves into the 30s. The family is now extended from 2 to 3 or 4. Additional expenses to up-bring the kids start kicking in. There is no thought about the money that needs to be allocated so that future goals are provisioned without any financial stress. The kid who was thrown into the water some years back is still struggling.

And then it becomes a lifestyle where whatever is earned is fully spent on bills, lifestyle, and loans, etc virtually with not enough money left to plan for essential goals. Any increment or promotion comes with increased expenses in the form of a higher standard of living. And this is where an individual or household gets stuck in the Rat Race Trap.

In this journey, they meet some financial agents who sell them financial products that can offer them tax rebates or some interest. Being financial illiterate they are not able to evaluate if the product suits their needs and they end up purchasing junks. Financial illiteracy and wrong money management further leave them lesser money. The only way that is left for them is to work harder so that they can make more money with the hope that they will get rid of financial stress that their current lifestyle has brought to them. Rat Race Trap continues.

It does not matter how much money you make. What matters is how much you are able to save, invest and grow.

Be proud of your income but your investments will make your pride.

Spending habits marks the fundamental difference between people in all earning patterns. As we stated earlier, very few are blessed to start right in the life journey in any earning pattern. But with proper money management, financial literacy, controlling spending habits and investing for growth is possible which eventually leads towards freedom from Rat Race Trap.

There is a nice quote from Mahatma Gandhi on the habits and its effect on our destiny.

> "Your beliefs become your thoughts,
> Your thoughts become your words,

Your words become your actions,
Your actions become your habits,
Your habits become your values,
Your values become your destiny."

Our thoughts and subsequent actions forms our habits and then knowingly and unknowingly we keep following those habits. We become ignorant as to how those habits are shaping our future and what is good and what is bad for us. Controlling Spending Habits thus goes a long way in defining your financial destiny.

Elephant Story

Have you ever wondered how a powerful elephant is tied only with a small weak chain in which the elephant can break easily? This happens because of the elephant's belief system which is built when he is small and weak. When the elephant baby is caught he is tied with a strong chain which he could not break with his baby strength. So he keeps on breaking it and at one stage accepts that I can't break this chain. That's where his belief is born that whatever I do I can't break open this chain and accepts to be tied with the same chain even if he becomes much stronger.

Likewise, we also create belief systems based on our experiences and continue with the same belief system even if the time changes. That's why many people still follow the old style of money management and investments even if the time has changed drastically and thus accept the Rat Race Trap as a way of life.

In the later part of this book, we will try and elaborate on the ways to come out of the Rat Race Trap.

Points to Ponder

- Your money management belief system plays a vital role in getting Freedom from Rat Race Trap.

- As time changes you need to change your investment style. There is a great possibility of getting into a Rat Race Trap following the same old style of Investment.

CHAPTER
Six

Rat Race Effects on Life

What happens when we are running a **race** or a marathon? In anticipation for the race to start, the stress hormone adrenaline increases and causes our heart rate to increase. Our brain will also send a signal to the lungs to increase the breathing. Crossing the finish line is a surreal feeling that we get to experience. The aches and pains that we experience during and after the race quickly subside and what is left behind is a wonderful feeling of fulfillment and happiness.

But **the Race** of Rat Race Trap that we are in does not have a finish line. Hence there is never a feeling of fulfillment. It negatively affects total well-being which impacts Family and Social Life. Runners of the Rat Race Trap can face some serious health issues due to heightened stress levels both at the physical and mental levels. Energy and enthusiasm levels become low. This unhappiness can impact the quality of life and can further shorten the lifespan as well. They are unable to think about the future as they can't see a finish line. It is illusive, blurred and uncertain.

When we are happy our life is fuelled by a sense of purpose and we gamely tackle each day, along with the challenges and goals we have set for ourselves. But when we are in a less fulfilling situation we accomplish less and less as the days drag on. It impacts our confidence, attitude, and urge to achieve something great in life. We feel powerless to adapt change or think there's nothing better out there. We start performing far below our true potential. We forget about ourselves, what really matters to us. We just keep running and get tired.

In the corporate culture, we frequently keep hearing about the term called 'Work-Life Balance'. It is a method which helps employees of an organization to balance their personal and professional lives. Encourages them to divide their time on the basis of priorities and maintain a balance by devoting time to family, health, vacations, etc along with making a career, business travel, etc.

Different people have different views about their work-life balance. These views are majorly driven by Rat Race Trap. When we interacted with an employee of a leading IT firm he expressed his emotions in the way below.

He says, "Work-Life Balance? , *does it really exist? Work-life Balance is a big Myth. It is the term coined by the corporate world to mislead us by creating a superficial sense of well-being and care for us by our employers. But the instances like skipping lunch to complete that coveted brand pitch or sacrificing our vacation to tend to a project or excusing our self from daughter's annual gathering to battle an office crisis aren't very uncommon.*

In hindsight, many of such instances can be handled smoothly in our absence or can be rescheduled. But it does not happen. We are too afraid to refuse or say No or ask for rescheduling. Our boss always remembers our one refusal and it reflects badly on our appraisals. The appraisal in corporate (especially in India) is also a very funny process. It is supposed to focus on our strengths and we are expected to be rated based on that. What happens, in reality, is the process focuses more on what we have not done rather than what we have done. More on our weakness and less on strengths. It is kind of an elimination process where the outperformer employees are selected by eliminating others. Another famous criterion that our boss applies during our appraisal is how much time we have spent in the office. The more you slog the better the chance that you may be rated higher.

Unlike the West, messages and emails on personal phones keep pinging and demand a response whether it's a holiday or off-duty hours. Most Indians are used to working 'beyond office-hours' and a refusal may come in the way of their annual appraisal. This need to 'sacrifice' has worsened with the digitally 'available' era, one lives in, today. You are on call 24x7. Where is 'Work-Life Balance' in all this mess?

And still, we are left with no option but to stick to the same job or profession. Sacrifice in a job is reflected in many ways, long commute, the intensity of the work, the pressures of the very role you are in, being on call when off-duty and the frequent travel demands.

Job Security, nowadays, is another common cause of stress. Companies expect us to be loyal during the booming job market. They will show all those carrots to us and will try to brainwash stating that it is not only the money that matters but loyalty as well. Loyalty towards the company will fetch us long term rewards. But the same employer, with the slightest hint of slowdown, will resort to cost control measures and we employees are the first casualty of it. Employees, especially at the mid-management level who are in their late 30s or 40s, are more vulnerable to layoffs, restructuring or management changes.

*So I feel that self-employment and business is the right solution for Work-Life Balance. Businessman and self-employed work as per their wish, as per their time. They have freedom of time with them. They have the freedom to decide their own pay package. They can enjoy time with family whenever they want. **I am planning to start my own business in the food industry or education.**"*

We interacted with many employees from different sectors and companies, more than 90% of them expressed similar emotions.

As a reality check when we interacted with a businessman he expresses his views that

"Being an employee is very good. In an organization, there is a system already in place. Every employee has to do only designated work. They need not worry about their paycheck at the end of the month. If the person is working in accounts he need not have to think about sales, marketing, production, delivery, transport, recovery, etc. He has to just keep the accounts. But that is not the case with me. I have to handle all these functions.

The customer/client is the king. They dictate terms to us. I have to manage my employees, vendors as well as my clients. The client's taste changes very fast. Coping up with the changing taste of the client is a difficult task. On top of that, there is a cut-throat competition in the market. There is a pressure 24/7 on my mind whether I can retain my client or not. We do not get skilled employees and as soon as they acquire skills they leave. Nowadays employee loyalty, as well as client loyalty, has gone down drastically due to the availability of various options. There is continuous pressure on profit margins.

There are no national Holidays. Only one day off in a week is allocated however I am not sure till that day whether I'll really be taking that day off or not. Many of the times I think what I am working for? Only to fulfill my and my family's monetary requirements but what about Time? Whether I am really living a life or just surviving? I can't even attend family functions and could not enjoy my kid's childhood.

All these things are creating a lot of stress in our community; this stress is affecting our physical and mental health. Nowadays blood pressure and heart problems are very common in our community.

As compared to employees life is better who get fixed pre-defined holidays, pre-defined weekly off, various types of paid leaves, pre-defined work time, pre-defined income, retirement benefits, bonus, increments."

From these 2 views do you remember the story of a cow that gets attracted towards a grassland on the other bank of the river? Which was greener compared to her grassland? One day she takes all the efforts to cross the river and reaches the greener grassland but she realized that grass on this land is the same as earlier one. Now when she looks back towards her earlier grassland from the other side of the bank of the river she feels that the earlier grassland is greener than where she is now.

So when we look towards the things being an outsider we may feel it is an easy and better option to be on the other side. But the reality may be totally different.

Actually, the problem is not how you are earning, how much you are earning. Whether you are an employee, a businessman, a self-employed professional or an investor. It's all about what you are missing in managing your hard-earned money. And because of that, you are already a Runner of a Rat Race Trap. The runners of Rat Race Trap cannot fulfill their materialistic commitments towards self and family. It creates stress on their mind which results in mental and physical disorders that affect every aspect of family, relationships, social, financial, career, self-esteem, the health of the Runner.

So the real solution is not in changing your style of earning, it's simply about adopting the right money management strategies to get freedom from Rat Race Trap.

Once you have the freedom from Rat Race Trap you will start loving your company, your job, your profession, your business, your employees, your friends, your colleagues and this world in all.

Think Hard – what it will take for you to come out of the Rat Race Trap?

Points to Ponder

- Is really the Grass greener on the other side?
- Earning pattern is not a root cause of you getting in the Rat Race Trap.
- Give careful consideration and adjust your viewfinder to life's priorities.

CHAPTER
Seven

Who is Responsible?

S teve Jobs famously used his 2005 Stanford University Commencement speech to say to the graduates in front of him: 'Your Time Is Limited. So Don't Waste It Living Someone Else's Life'.

Our beliefs and behaviors are first formed by influential adults in our life, like our parents or teachers. They make us believe that we need to follow their concepts to be successful or happy in life. It becomes a problem in adulthood because those concepts aren't relevant anymore. They want us to study hard, get a good job, get a house, get married, have kids, buy a car... get settled and goes on. There is nothing wrong with this because this is what they have also followed.

In India, due to improper education system, we have so many literate unemployment. And we are molded by our education system. There are so many people who are educated even holding a Ph.D. degree but are unemployed, or they are getting the job but it is not relevant to their qualifications. We have created this market economy that deforms us into other professions. The economy is connected to every person of the nation how every citizen makes money and flow that money.

So the options people normally choose are like

1. Either join a traditional concept of life by accepting that Rat Race Trap is part of life

2. Or change your earning style with an expectation that it will give you freedom from Rat Race Trap

3. Or you marry money and manage big businesses.

4. Or you work for the church, NGO

5. Or you go to the Himalayas where you are away from all the materialistic things.

None of these options is going to work. Unfortunately, most people do not know what right strategy they have to follow to get freedom from the rat race trap.

Most of us choose option 1. We can't go away from the materialistic world that's why Option 5 of going to the Himalayas is irrelevant. Money is needed for every small or big thing and the Rat Race Trap starts.

We are also influenced or impacted by what our peers or our neighbors or our relatives are doing. The peer pressure sometimes compels us to do the things even though it may not make much financial sense or we may not even need them.

My friend bought a new mobile. My mobile is also old and nowadays became slow (This mobile getting slow is more of perception though. Our mind is in search of some valid excuse) let me change it. The neighbor got a new car. Suddenly your car starts giving trouble and you feel it's time for you as well to upgrade the car.

"We buy things we don't need, with money we don't have, to impress people we don't like."

—Dave Ramsey

The media bombards us with their products and manipulates us to buy their products. We see thousands of direct or indirect advertisements every moment that we don't even realize it. We buy things we don't need and we go in debt. We Make Someone Else Rich. We don't save enough, we don't invest enough. We are not prepared for unexpected emergencies.

We Borrow, Borrow, and Borrow some more. Instead of buying only what we can afford, many of us simply continue to borrow more money to pay for the things we desire.

We get educated but still Financially Illiterate. Money isn't taught often in schools at any level. If you never learned how money works, how do you think you will be able to capture a large amount of it? Education systems are to produce clerks and not entrepreneurs. We were taught from a very young age that the only real way to make a living was through a job. There are some great products and ideas that have been stifled by a fear of risk-taking.

We Don't Learn. We are content to watch hours of TV Serials instead of picking up a book every once in a while. Intelligence solves problems. **The more you learn the more you can potentially earn.**

We are in a constant cycle of going to work and paying bills. The root of this is a lack of education, as well as the influence of the media, which is driven by consumerism. The idea of how members of our society are supposed to live is pre-determined. Until we identify what needs to be fixed, we can't make a change.

Points to Ponder

- We are brainwashed into a certain way of living.
- It's not a life requirement to follow the cycle of Rat Race Trap.
- The choice is completely up to us. But we need to notice our thoughts and feelings, and sorting them out to see which ones we need to let go of.

CHAPTER
Eight

Is there An Exit to Rat Race?

Let us remind you of a story known as "Frog in the well". There was a Frog who has always lived in the well from generation to generation. He had not seen the world outside his Well and never bothered to step out of it. He used to think his well is the biggest. One day a new Frog from the Sea travels and jumps into that well. The Frog in the Well asks the guest Frog where he is from. So the guest frog starts talking about the sea. Further enquiring he asks whether the sea is bigger than this well? Guest frog tells him it's much much bigger than this well. So the Frog in the well starts showing him the size by swimming from one end to the other and asks him if the sea is this big. Every time the Guest Frog refuses. Even after knowing that sea is bigger than the well, Frog in the well refuses to accept that Sea could be bigger than the well and continues to stay in the well and refuses to go out.

From the story, we come to know that it's important to first acknowledge the problem exists and then look for the solution. As read in the earlier chapter, our Rat in the Trap is also like this Frog in the Well who refuses to accept the fact and stay there forever not looking for a solution outside.

It's very important that you first acknowledge that you are in the Rat Race Trap. A solution can only be sought if there is an acceptance of the problem.

There goes a saying – 'Your life does not get better by chance, it gets better by change'

To reach the right solution, you first need to identify why this happens again and again with you. Unless and until you know the reason you will not get the right answer. It requires serious introspection. Introspect as to why every solution comes with a new problem. Maybe you are not solving the real problem but just covering it up with some short cut? Eventually making the original problem bigger & bigger.

Are you ready to go in an uncomfortable zone? Are you ready to make efforts for the lifestyle changes? Are you ready to change your habits? Are you ready to take your own responsibility? If the answer to these questions is yes, then yes there is an exit to Rat Race Trap.

You may be the only person who is looking for this change. Your parents would never have complained about this Rat Race Trap because the things were different at that time. Their expenses were much less than what they earned. And their habits were not expensive.

- They had a pension, job security and they had saved enough for their retirement.

- They had multiple Kids to ensure that someone will take care of them in their retirement.

- They had bare minimum expenses. They won't go frequently for luxury dining or vacations.

- They need not have to pay a high donation, school fees, or tuition fees for the education of their children

- They used public transport or walk, whereas kids use luxury travel, Uber or Ola.

- Essentially there were not many avenues to spend money. Now there are many.

You have good earning capacity. Your expenses are not much. You have even saved & invested a part of your income. Then why you still are in this Rat Race Trap?

Is this what you are wondering all the time then, it clearly means that what you are doing right now is not right and you have to change something.

Now the question is where and what you are missing? And your answer is - "You are missing at your financial management strategies." Your wrong financial management strategies are the real cause of your Rat Race Trap.

Or we can say that you are using the wrong financial management techniques rightly.

Everyone taught us how to earn money, but how to plan and use the earned is not taught.

Even that is fine. But what you have done thereafter? Nothing.

Do you really care about your money? No? Then will money take care of you? If you have not empowered and nurtured your money to work as hard as you, then why will it be like, you want it to be?

What we have observed is people earn money to become Rich and Invest to become Poor. The wrong financial Management strategies which you follow, helps you to get into the Rat Race Trap, and we call these strategies as the Best ways to become Poor.

Sometimes the people are so ignorant that they are not even aware that there is a problem. And be mindful that overcoming of Rat Race Trap does not happen overnight. There is no magic wand or formula that will turn your financial fortunes overnight. It may be a bit troublesome in the beginning as it may need you to give up some luxuries or make some lifestyle compromises. But once you start thinking long term and visualize how your life could be, you will eventually start enjoying it. It will teach you new experiences, will develop your personality. Life will be fun. And that's the ultimate aim of Rat Race Trap Freedom.

Let's first find out what all can go wrong and how one can take control to make it right.

In the next section of this book, we will discuss where and what you might have missed and in the last section we will discuss the solution, it's a deal.

Are you ready? Before we start with the next section, this is what we would want you to do. Make a list of things you have been doing till now, and as and when that same thing appears in the book, you should tick that in your list too. So that you can check which areas you need to work on.

Points to Ponder

- Introspect the situation that you are in.

- Accept if you are really in the problem.

- Accept that no one else is going to find a solution for yourself, it's your responsibility to find a solution to the problem.

- And take a short term pain to implement the solution for your Rat Race trap Freedom.

PART
Two

Traps

We already have discussed, what the Rat Race Trap is. Now you know that, people are unaware about financial management or financially illiterate, they normally follow the same strategies which leads them to RRT. This part let's take a tour to why RRT happens?

Let's discuss some of these wrong money management strategies which we call as **Best ways to become poor.**

CHAPTER
One

Trap of Income and Expenses

1st 10 days

2nd 10 days

last 10 days

If we save today, we will be rich tomorrow.

> *"Insanity is doing the same thing over and*
> *over again and expecting different results."*
>
> **—Albert Einstein'**

Many people don't understand how to manage income and expenses. Till now it was ok but since you have set yourself to the path of Rat Race Freedom, you have to learn something new; you have to try something different. Essentially if you want different results than what you're getting, you have to try different approaches.

Let's further delve into this.

2 common rules are widely used to depict the relationship between income, expenses, and savings (which goes to investments).

Rule No.1

INCOME - EXPENSES = SAVINGS
(Which will go to INVESTMENT)

This rule is followed by people who are always seeking instant gratification. Spending takes priority over saving. Whatever they are earning they will spend on Needs (mandatory expenses like EMI, Utility bills, Grocery, etc.) as well as want (Shopping, Dining, Vacations, Clubs, etc.). If there is something left after pampering to self, spouse (&/or boyfriend/ girlfriend) and kids then that becomes their saving. There is no question of investing here because these people hardly understand the concept of investing and hence the need for the same. Remember - **here saving may happen by chance and not by choice**.

These are kind of people with typical attitude as 'कल किसने देखा'. They claim that they are living in the present and there is no need to worry about the future as the future is unknown and uncertain.

But the reality with most of such people who follow this rule is, they live like king for the first 10 days after receiving their monthly paycheque, next 10 days will be like the middle class and last 10 days like a ...., They live a life on borrowings. Borrowing either through credit cards or from friends and relatives (if they are lucky to have someone from whom they have not borrowed before). Sooner they will find themselves in a situation where they have no friend left who can lend them, their credit cards are exhausted and they get hopelessly trapped in an RRT where there is no hope of any freedom.

Are you one of those people who are following this rule? Are you the one who is obsessed with instant gratification? Are you the one who gets an adrenaline rush and feels superhuman after spending? If you are, then there is a great chance that you are already in RRT or you are on borderline.

Rule No.2

INCOME – SAVINGS (INVESTMENTS) = EXPENSES.

To find people living with this formula we don't have to go too far. The example is present in our house itself. Most of our parents always made us save first from whatever we got and then spend the rest; they followed the same rule. Even Warren Buffet says that it is a good way to save and invest but still you will find these people in an RRT.

How come? What wrong they are doing or have they not understood what saving means? We have seen our parents always being worried about the future. They hardly have enjoyed their present just because they had to save first. We have seen them compromise their lives, needs, wants & desires for the sake of the future and no one knows when that future will come.

Don't we know many people who love this rule? They say that this is the ideal rule which every individual should follow. Are they right? Sorry, we do not recommend this rule at all.

Shocking? Do you know what the problem in this rule is?

This rule will make you compromise your today; you may not be able to enjoy your today. Whenever the expenses come you will always think of saving. **You may be earning handsome but living like poor.**

The reality is, once you tune into compromising your life, you will just earn money for the sake of saving, and may not utilize the money for yourself. If you compromise your today, you won't be happy even if you act like you are happy. If you are not happy today you may not enjoy your tomorrow also. The irony is that whatever the wealth these people acquire over their lifetime by living like a peasant, someone else enjoys their wealth.

Why you are saving, for your tomorrow? When that tomorrow will come? For most such people, it doesn't come because "tomorrow never dies". Tomorrow is a horizon which will be always far from you. So, the question is why and whom are you earning for? Such money is of no use. If you are following this rule then you are not right. Even if you have a lot of money still the sad part of it is that you could not realize your created wealth. Then what's the use?

So, both of these rules which are used commonly leads to RRT.

Rule no. 1 is not right because it will ruin your future. You may not be left with sufficient money to fulfill your future needs, requirements and financial goals.

Rule no. 2 is also not right because if you are a follower of this rule you may not be happy today. You are just compromising your life with a dream of making your tomorrow better which nobody knows whether it will come or not. **Keep in mind "If you are not happy today, you cannot enjoy your future."**

Now your question would be "what to do?". Wait the answer is coming for you....

Points to Ponder

- Analyze your income expenses style. Which rule you fall in.

- To enjoy your future, you should be happy today.

- Those who are happy today and prepared for the future only can get freedom from Rat Race Trap.

CHAPTER
Two

Do You Know Your Enemy No. 1?

Imagine you are at a war, where you don't know who is your enemy, you don't know his strength, you don't even know how well he is prepared, and so you don't know how to fight.

Who will win the war? You? Very least possibility.

Most of us don't even know that we are already at a war, a war of wealth creation. There is our enemy who is fighting against us day and night, 24 hrs. a day, 365 days a year. Our enemy does not rest, does not stop, nor takes holidays. In fact, when we are on holiday or leave, we increase his power.

This war will continue throughout our life, till our death, our enemy will die with us only. We can win over him but can't kill him, he is going to stay but we can make him ineffective, we can make him surrender. He is not in our control, but yes, we can make him ineffective by having an army more powerful than him. He will then remain suppressed throughout your life.

If we could not have a stronger Army then he will make us, surrender, he is already made many lives a nightmare. **We are sure some of you might have started guessing this enemy.**

Yes, it's Inflation

Inflation? Do you really understand it? Do you know how really it affects you?

There are many people around us who keep suggesting to invest in PF, FDs, Post office schemes, traditional insurance, etc. But these people are not a financial expert. And very few of them understand the concept of inflation-adjusted returns*. Had they understood the inflation probably they would not have advised investing all or most of your money in FDs or PFs. They just want to cut down your expenses and what they know is PF, FD's, Post office schemes, traditional insurance, etc. Compulsory savings instruments. But they don't know that just saving is not enough beating inflation is. The vehicle that they suggest may end up providing us zero or worst negative inflation-adjusted return.

So now our new goal is to understand the inflation

"Definition"

Inflation is the rate at which the general level of prices for goods and services is rising and, consequently, the purchasing power of the money is falling (To buy the same item you have to pay more money year after year). Central banks attempt to limit inflation in order to keep the economy running smoothly. As per RBI's latest data, current inflation in India is around 4% to 5% (References).

Inflation Increases Cost of Products

	Loaf of Bread	1 Ltr Milk	1 Ltr Petrol	Higher Education
2000	10	25	28	3 lakhs
2030*	51	129	265	47 lakhs

Assuming Inflation 6%

Ref 2.1

Next is a million-dollar question, if your answer to this question is wrong then take it from us that you are marching towards RRT or you are already in an RRT.

The question: What is the rate of inflation?

Many people are in a wonderland of the economy come with answers like inflation is abound 4%, 5%, 8% not only you but many so-called financial planners also take inflation in the same range.

What they fail to understand that, we are living in inflationary and one of the fastest-growing countries like India. We are not in a developed country like the US, Australia, Germany where the rate of inflation is stabilized and is typical does not cross the figure of 2% to 4%. One more thing normal person understands inflation which is declared by Govt. Of India based on CPI (References). This inflation is only 1 effect. Normally inflation is considered as price rise, which is correct as per textbook definition, but this does not have the right meaning in your life.

"Personal Inflation"

Do you feel that your expense has gone much higher than what experts are claiming? Go through calculations and find it yourself. Is your inflation rate being the same as 6%-8% like what others are saying?

Note that your personal inflation is a rise in personal expenses year after year.

Inflation rate = % of the change in expense amount year after year.

Let us understand this with a simple calculation, **the rule of 72**.

How to calculate expenses doubling period if you know the rate of inflation:

If you divide 72 with the rate of inflation, the result will be no of years in which your expenses will go double.

Let's consider the rate of inflation is 6%. Then 72/6=12. So, it means that your expenses would go double in 12 years. (This is too long! Do your expenses take this long to get double?)

How to calculate the rate of inflation if you know expenses doubling period:

If you divide 72 with no of years in which your expenses got double then you will get the rate of inflation.

e.g. If your expense got double in 8 years then to calculate the rate of inflation 72/8=9. So, the rate of inflation is 9% in this case.

Now coming back to reality.

Your expenses are doubled in the last 5 years, which means your rate of inflation is ~ 14.5%.

Your expenses are doubled in the last 6 years, which means your rate of inflation is ~ 12%.

Shocked...? I know, but true.

Don't get panic it might have happened because you got married recently, you might have changed your lifestyle; you might have a baby in your family. This high rate of inflation is because of these effects but soon it will come down to 10% to 11%.

Now you have a question in your mind how come the rate of inflation of government is different from my rate of inflation?

Here is an explanation for you. First, you need to understand that the rise in your personal, family expenses is inflation for you.

Let's understand what are the contributors in your expense, it's not only price rise.

When you are in the accumulation phase your expenses move northwards because of 3 major effects.

1. The normal price rise in the market (Basic inflation)

2. The change in the choice (This is a major contributor) these are lifestyle expenses that contribute to 30%-50% of the part of your total expenses.

3. Increase in unit consumption.

LifeStyle Inflation

Your choice decides your expenses.

Most people love to increase their standard of living. A person earning 50k a month would love to spend like someone who is earning 75k a month. And that is but natural. Human life is always evolving and in a constant search of more comforts and luxuries.

Item	*Ordinary Product*	*Branded Product*	*% Increase in Inflation*
Shoes	500	3000	600%
Watch	500	10000	2000%
Restaurant	500	6000	1200%
School Fees	25000	150000	600%
Mobile	5000	20000	400%
Two-Wheeler	50000	350000	700%
Movie in theatre	100	400	400%
Vacation	50000	120000	240%

Ref 2.2

The flip side of this human nature is that you need not have to take the effort to increase your expenses; it will take care of its own.

One question we normally ask in our sessions is - Who knows first that your salary is increased, you have got a bonus or you have got an increment or incentive?

All married men in session reply: My Wife :).

But it's not true. The first one to know is "Your expenses". It has all the senses what we have. Once expenses know that the money is coming, it makes a plan and intimates your wife and other family members.

Jokes apart, but it's true! Have you taken any efforts to date to increase your Expenses? We know your answer: "No"! We know your expenses grow without your permission. Lifestyle is a major contributor to increasing your Inflation.

Increase in unit consumption

When you are young, you are alone and hence you have to spend only on self-expense. When you get married, then all requirements, including your basic necessities almost get doubled. Once you have a child some new requirements along with an increase in units of basic necessities. For e.g. If you need ½ lit Milk before marriage, you require 1 lit after and 1.5 lit or 2 lit once you have a child. So not only price rise in milk had affected your expense but the demand in your family as well.

Because of these 3 effects, your expense increases and are not in tune with government declared figures. It would be much higher.

Essentially your expenses are going up by 10% to 12% (& maybe more) every year and your investments are growing at what rate? What kind of returns you are getting from legacy investment options like PPF, FDs or Traditional Insurance policies?

Here you have to understand if your total investment portfolio is giving returns less than what your inflation then you are fighting a losing battle. With each passing year, you are becoming poor because your earnings are not able to keep pace with inflation and result in increased expenses.

If now you can't build an army stronger than your enemy then that's foolish, right?

I hope you will understand why all those people who felt inflation was around 6-8% and invest in instruments with the return of 7-9%. But these people don't know that they were **investing to become poor.** It was because they were playing to lose ……. Get...set...Go....

Another concept you must understand is about: **Amount and Value.**

The amount is Different and Value is different.

Let us take an example.

Let's say you have ₹100 Rs today. Also, assume that you want to purchase item 'A' after one year which is also currently costing ₹100. As you don't want to buy this product today and have that money in your pocket, you can keep it like that or invest in traditional instruments. Now think about what happens after one year.

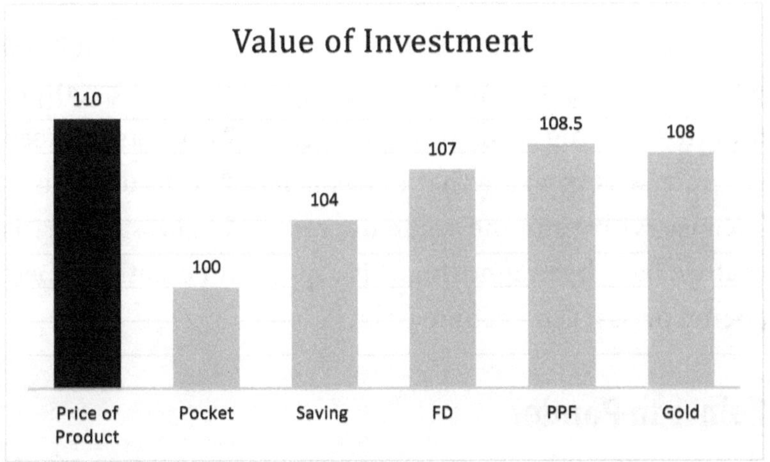

Ref 2.3

From this result, you understand that the product which you can buy as on today with the money in your pocket you may not be able to buy in the next year, even if you had invested that money in options you think is best. So actually, these investments made you poor.

This is the difference in amount and value.

Value is the purchasing power of money. If you can maintain the purchasing power of the money you are maintaining the value of money.

I hope this example will come as an eye-opener. By now you should know what you are doing with your money. The options which you have chosen are making you Rich or Poor? So simple rule to become Rich is, your portfolio should deliver returns more than the rate of inflation (your personal inflation and not the government declared inflation).

Remember when the generation of 80's said that ₹100 was such a big amount that having a salary of ₹100 per month was a big deal. Today that same ₹100 has reduced so much less in value that it seems like ₹10 to us. This is because with time the value depreciated. The sad part is that we have been ignoring this aspect and creating a best enemy or asset to become poor.

Points to Ponder

- If you do not know what inflation is you might already be very close to Rat Race Trap or already in it.

- Inflation declared by the government and personal inflation is different.

- Use Rule 72 to calculate your personal inflation.

- To know the amount required in the future for your financial goals always use your personal inflation.

CHAPTER
Three

*Do Not Understand the Time
Value of Money*

There is a famous advertisement of a branded perfume which shows when a pilot walks in the cabin his co-pilot says "Bad morning. Flight is delayed by 30 minutes". Upon hearing this pilot makes an announcement that the flight is delayed by 3 hours. All passengers are nervous, angry, frustrated.

After few minutes the pilot makes an updated announcement, "Good news to all the passengers. The flight is about to take off in just 30 minutes". All passengers obviously relieved and turn happy". And then the pilot tells his co-pilot, that there are only good mornings.

How easily he managed to break this news to the passenger turning their anger or uneasiness to wait for more 30 minutes into a happy 30-minute delay, by fooling them in a smart way that they didn't understand.

This is what happens in the financial sector too. They give some hope of acquiring an X amount in Y years but in reality due to time factor you may lose the value of that amount by Z %.

And you feel proud that your investment got you good returns simply because you don't really understand the time value in investment. Just like the pilot knew that in reality the flight is been delayed only by 30 minutes, but passengers didn't know, so he could use this smart trick to avoid making them feel sad about the delay. In the same way the financial products salesperson knows that your future value of current investment will not match up with increasing inflation, but he knows this too that you don't really know what time value of money is. So, he uses that to his benefit and pitches you his product which may give some average return, but not the needed value on that investment

Today ₹100 is more valuable than ₹100 after 1 year, right? Why?

Great you reached to right answer,you are smart. You read in enemy no 1:Inflation. In the inflationary economy the purchasing power of money goes down year after year, the value of money devaluates. So from this simple example, you know that there is a value associated with Money, you also now know that there is a difference between Value and Amount.

You can easily calculate value of ₹100 one year down the line by assuming certain inflation rate and by using simple mathematical calculations. But when the calculation is for 5, 10 or more years, it becomes a bit complex. This is where the real trap lies. Since you are unable to calculate / visualize value of ₹100 over a period of time, you fail as a buyer and end up purchasing a ninvestment instrument whose value may go into negative on maturity. This is how sellers gain.

Let's take an example. Suppose there is a product that requires you to invest only ₹10,000 per year for 30 years. On maturity you will get 3 times what you had invested. i.e. On investment of 3 lac you get ₹9 lacs on maturity. Sounds great?

But not really, in % terms your compounded annual returns will be hardly 6.38%. Same or less than what your FD offers. And if there is a tax element attached to it then value of your investment will further erode and you may end up in negative value for your investment after 30 years.

So, on the face of it, these investment looks really great, really attractive. Figure of ₹9 lacs really looks too big today. but since you could not calculate how much the value of that ₹9 lac after 30 years will be, you fall in this trap, in the trap of becoming poor.

Real Rate of Return

This leads us to the interesting concept of Real Rate of Return. The rate of interest that you earn on your investment and the resultant amount at the time of maturity is different than the value of maturity (Value of money at maturity). We saw this just now. So, if we have to calculate the real value of money at the time maturity you need to calculate the Real rate of return. In other words,you have to calculate inflation-adjusted rate of return.

If inflation adjusted return is less than 0 (Negative) means you had chosen investments which are making you poor, the value of money is going down.

If inflation adjusted return is equal to 0 it means the investment you had chosen at least maintained the value of money.

If inflation adjusted return is bigger than 0, means positive, then the investment you had chosen is making you rich.

The maturity amount of money is more valuable than the money which you had invested. Such type of investments is smart investments, oh! Don't ask us immediately which are these investments? Yes, we know and we are going to tell you but that is in the Solution section, not now.

Now how you can calculate the real rate of return. The formula for same is

$$((1 + r)/(1 + i) - 1) \times 100$$

Where

r = Rate of Return

i = Rate of Inflation

Now you can just calculate all your investments which you have today whether they qualify to become Rich or poor.

For long term investment calculation, you go to Excel and use function of Future value (FV).

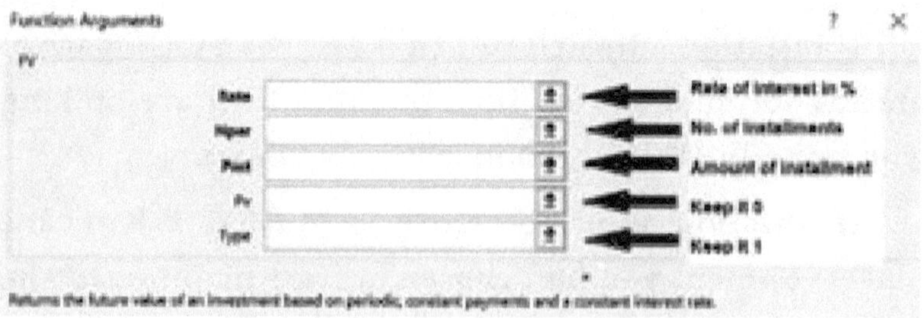

Now don't do any mental calculation or just to get an idea to refer to Table 1 in Annexure.

Use Table 1 in Annexure to cross verify, when anyone comes to you and promises a return.

We are sure most of the investment product sellers come to you for selling investment products, irrespective of what they call themselves, also would not know these calculations.

Henceforth if you don't want to lose the value of your money, Stay - in, for next coming section, where we will see how to make this time value of money work in your favor and to make your life Rich and Happy.

Points to Ponder

- Investment's inflation-adjusted return <0, then your investments are making you poor.

- Investment's inflation-adjusted return = 0, then your investments are not taking you anywhere.

- Investment's inflation-adjusted return >0, then your investments are making you RICH.

CHAPTER
Four

Do You Know Your Enemy No. 2?

TAX

> *"There are only 2 things which are certain
> in this world; Death and Tax."*
>
> **—Benjamin Franklin**

How do you feel when you earn handsome but actually what comes in your hands is handsome minus tax? The tax takes away your earnings every time in many different ways. Tax is your enemy on the journey of becoming wealthy. It's not only about direct income tax but there are other indirect taxes also which you are paying every time. So you pay the tax at the time of earning as well as at the time of spending. These indirect taxes are GST, Toll, Property Tax, Water Tax, State and Central Taxes (e.g. tax you pay on fuel like diesel or petrol). Yes, I know it's painful. But….

Hey! Congratulations to you if you are paying taxes!!

If you paying taxes means you are one among those fortunate people who have their income in the taxable range and you are having a lifestyle that almost 80 to 90% of the world population can't even think of.

Taxes are good. It is the treasure used by the government to spend on the developmental activities so that the country keeps progressing and hence it's citizens. The money spent gives us access to better education, infrastructure, healthcare and hence results in providing more employment and business opportunities. People get more and more avenue where they create more money and keep improving their standard of living. So far so good.

Then what's wrong? It is not saving tax but saving tax with wrong investment instruments.

Just like we all get bombarded with lots of product and advertisements and fall prey to buying such unwanted things, same happens with tax-related policies or schemes, most of the people buy products of which they have heard or seen the most, rather than buying those that shall help them the fullest.

Many people think that tax consideration is important only at the time of earning, salary, business or professional charges. Well, that's not true in its entirety. You have to think about tax treatment at the time of investments as well. At the time of starting investment and also at the time of investment getting matured.

There is a season for tax saving in India. It starts in the last 3 months of the end of the financial year. Normally people start thinking about investments as a reaction to pay less tax or when they get an mail from their employer mentioning the last date to submit investment proofs towards the end of the financial year. All people then have only 1 thing on top of their mind, how to save maximum tax? And here they fall in the trap. The trap of tax-saving investments.

This is where most of the people fail prey to. People have only one purpose for investments, Tax Saving. **Tax**

saving the wrong financial goal. To save tax they will do all kinds of disorganized purchases and that too in a wrong investment instrument. To save tax they will buy a house that comes with all its expenses of buying and maintaining it, or traditional insurance policies like an endowment plan or FDs which give negative inflation-adjusted returns. The investments are so random, so disorganized and with every passing year, one keeps investing in some or other new instruments which ultimately makes it difficult to keep the track of where all one has invested and what benefits one is getting out of it.

No doubt, tax saving is important but you should not forget your enemy no. 1(Inflation). The maximum investment made for tax saving makes you poor. The non-targeted investments can erode your hard-earned wealth. Also, if you have invested in an instrument with a higher lock-in periods of 10-15 years (like PPF), then you may not be in a position to fully liquidate them when there is a need where the money is required to meet some financial goal. Beware of the Tax Trap where one keeps investing to save tax at the cost of sacrificing some financial goals.

You already know this, but we want to repeat it again and again for your benefit. **If you don't take care of your hard-earned money, someone else will use it for their ultimate benefit.** They will sell the stuff to you which is extremely harmful to your financial health but immensely beneficial for them.

Ask a question to yourself, why someone else will take care of your money? Find an answer for this, and we will invest more time on this question in our next trap. Salaried individuals should understand, they can't save tax more than a specific limit. There are limited options available.

Refer to Table 4.1. There we have listed some of the tax-saving instruments(80C) and its approximate returns. This table can help you to analyze better the tax-saving instruments that you have chosen are making you RICH and POOR.

Tax Saving Instruments(80C)	*Personal Inflation* adjusted Return*
PF	~ -1.5%
ELSS (Tax saving Mutual Funds)	~ +2%
PPF	~ -2 %
Sukanya Samruddhi	~ -2 %
NSC	~ -1.5%
Bank FDs (Tax Saving)	~ -3 %
Insurance	~ -6 to -5%
*Personal inflation at 10%. (Refer to Enemy no. 1)	

Table 4.1

Housing Loan Tax Saving Trap:

There is one more trap created with the help of tax-saving consideration.

It's a tax-saving by taking the housing loan. If you take a housing loan then there are 2 tax benefits you can avail.

U/S 80C against the principle paid and U/S 24B against interest paid for a housing loan.

All salaried individuals are already paying PF which is also a part of 80C. If your PF contribution is high then your 80C limit may be already exhausted, what you can get is only 24B. Many people feel that it is a benefit. I am saving tax and thus I am making a sensible decision. Yes, it is a sensible decision if it's your first home which you bought because you want to stay in it. But for 2nd home is it still a sensible decision? We will discuss it separately in points later.

Now a statement we are going to make may shake your thought process and you may have to read this sentence once again.

"You have to take a loss to take 24B tax benefit and the loss would be higher than benefit"

As of today the maximum limit of section 24B is ₹2,00,000 a year. But most people fail to understand that, this ₹2,00,000 is an interest paid to the bank against your housing loan. So actually, most of the amount out of ₹2,00,000 is your loss. You can save tax as per tax bracket only.

So, if you paid ₹2,00,000 interest what you can save in tax is as follows:

At 10% bracket, the tax saved is ₹20,000 a year, so the loss is ₹ 1,80,000.

At 20% bracket, the tax saved is ₹ 40,000 a year, so the loss is ₹ 1,60,000.

At 30% bracket, the tax saved is ₹ 60,000 a year, so the loss is ₹ 1,40,000.

This loss also takes a portion of the appreciation of property. And the other trap of Risk is you may end up having a real estate tilted portfolio. Many people already are experiencing real estate risk since 2014. Properties they hold are not delivering good rental income and if they want to sell, there are no buyers at the right price in the market, facing a liquidity crunch. **On paper they are RICH but by pocket they are POOR.** This may be harmful to your financial health which may take you to Rat Race Trap.

In the next section, we shall go in detail and find a solution for coming out of the tax trap and for newbie of how not to get into the Trap in the first place.

Points to Ponder

- After reading and observing plus interviewing many people, we could draw 3 basic reasons for falling in a tax trap.

- Taxpayers buy investments just to save tax without linking it to any of their future financial goals.

- They also don't understand the returns that this investment instrument is going to give them and whether it will be able to beat the inflation. They are absolutely in the dark about what they are going to do with this saved money.

- They buy in a hurry before the last date of the financial year so they don't get time to check what they are buying and why what will be its use. There only ultimate goal is to save the tax. Like we get glued to ads and buy things even if we don't need them, the same happens with tax, we see others buying it, so we follow the herd.

CHAPTER
Five

Debt Trap

DEBT
TRAP

We all are in search of happiness. Almost all of us try to find that happiness in materialistic possessions. For that we often shop. We believe that the things we buy will make us happier ("An Idea can change your life"), confident ("Jiyo Sir UthaKe") and respectable ("The Complete Man"). We attach our self-worth and our social status to the things that we own. A well-furnished House, A luxury Car, Expensive jewelry, Elite Club membership are some of the things we crave for to increase our self-esteem. We always want something better, something bigger than what our neighbor, friend or colleague may have.

We shop for cosmetics, hair treatments, and weight loss products to enhance physical self. We shop for attractive clothes to improve our self-confidence. We shop for few products like washing machines, freeze, smartphones or GPS to make our life easier. Or we shop for books, CDs or recreational activities to add pleasure in our lives. We hope that these materialistic things will transform our lives and we keep on spending money on these.

The homemaker feels that she should have her home neat and clean. If friends/neighbors and relatives see untidy clothes then that will leave a bad impression of her. When asked about it to our female client she said "But if I do the interior and design beautiful a wardrobe it will hide my untidy clothes and home will look clean that will give a good first impression. If I have a bigger house to show off to my friends, I'll improve my image, will have a better relationship with them and will command more respect. If I buy those expensive toys for my kids, it will keep them engaged and allow me more free time. Also, I can boast it to the other parents by showing as to how well I have taken care of my kids."

By doing this we feel that we can get more respect, acknowledgment from society and will further boost our self-esteem and make us happy.

The flip side is - This search for happiness makes us more and more greedy. Sooner than later we forget the boundary between **WANTS** and **NEEDS** we start spending recklessly. We start cluttering our life and space with the things that we either use very rarely or we don't need.

Look at your wardrobe and you will find that expensive *ghagra* or *silk sari* or *paithani* lying somewhere in the corner of the wardrobe, and now fading, which you had worn only once during your marriage or reception. The same is true for gents. Those 3 pieces have become useless because they have now both grown in size and weight. This is just one example. You will find many such things - right from unwanted furniture, to showpieces, to clothes that you had purchased some year back to get that instant zing of self-gratification. The cluttering of life and space, in fact, adds more stress because shopping is one time but maintenance becomes lifelong.

This shopping mania gets us into the debt trap if we let our emotions take complete control of ourselves. The craving of more and more forces us to take the loans. Your bank balance starts suffering, you start digging all your savings and you even compromise on that investment which is supposed to be for your child education or retirement. Once you exhaust these avenues then you look for personal loans, car loans, loans from friends & families or credit cards (will come in the next chapters). Eventually, you find yourself in the debt trap and start living on the borrower's life. Some genius creatures around us take another loan to pay the previous outstanding loan.

I. What is a debt trap?

In the past 10-15 years with the rise in income (Disposable income: Retail industry coined this term to tune your mind to dispose of your savings at their counters) and hence consumption, one can get loan easily for almost anything and everything. Also, due to the constant advertisement all over the place, one tends to over-leverage the income by buying things on loan, easily available. Sales strategies are designed in such a way that we as a consumer do not initially feel the pinch in terms of financial outgo, however, the total outgo over time including the interest amount sometimes is more than twice or thrice the cost of the product. It's like – ज़ोर का झटका धीरे से लगे.

Some companies offer zero percent loans for the purchase of consumer durables such as TV, smartphones, Freeze, etc. But are these zero percent loan? During the start of festive seasons, you would have opted for 'No-cost EMI' or 'Zero Cost EMI' on products like mobile phones, electronic appliances, and so on. Did you ever wonder how this works? This is a marketing gimmick. One should remember that there is always a cost that one has to bear because you know that there are no Free lunches in the world. Here either the interest amount is added to the product price or a discount is equivalent to interest or you pay the processing fees. In some cases, the interest rate may work out in such loans is usually very high ranging between 16 percent and 24 percent. And just try defaulting one payment and you will know the gimmick behind this zero percent.

When you take a loan, you are leveraging your future income for present consumption which is a very risky thing to do. At one end, companies launch new products and on the other hand, there are ready loans available at very high rates of interest. And you fall for those products. No matter how much you try, you can't pay off these debts. It keeps multiplying as interest piles on. You are unable to keep track of these loans, outstanding and interests. Make irregular payments whenever there is some money. You got stuck in a vicious cycle and this precisely is called a debt trap bringing constant stress and anxiety over your capability to service the loan obligations.

And over time, as the 2008 recession showed us, when things turn worse, people start faltering on their loan payments, which start impacting their credit score & worse, results in repossession of house/car etc. by the financing company which becomes a big source of emotional loss & can even lead one to depression.

Points to Ponder

- Rise in income and falling for sales strategies may lead to a bad habit of spending money on unnecessary items.

- This bad habit gets you into a debt trap due to Easy Loans.

CHAPTER
Six

Credit Card - A Trap

PAY
UP
CRED
9000
Hug

Most of us own a credit card, maybe one, two or more. The financial institutes that issue you the credit card, give it to you for free. There is no charge for the same. Have you ever thought about how these banks or financial institutes can afford to give a Free Credit card? (Do you know: Its free only in the first year. Next year onwards there are annual charges.) They are obviously not in the market for charity with a noble cause of supporting you financially. They are in the market to earn revenue and profit. And after all, we all know - ***'There is no such a thing called a free meal.'***

If you do not have an answer to these questions, miss one or two of the credit card installments and you will be penalized in more than one way.

First, you will be levied the late fee charges.

Second, you will have to pay the penalty on the outstanding balance with a ridiculously high-interest rate. The rate can be as high as 1.25% to 3.5%+per month i.e. around 15%to 42%+ per annum compounded monthly. Add late fee charges to this it becomes approx. 50%.

Credit Card loans are the highest interest rates loans legally available in the market. Sometimes it's even more than the "Sahukari Loans" available in the market. Compare it with interest rate on the savings account which is around 4% or Fixed Deposits interest rate which is 6% and you will realize that how brutally you are been charged for not settling the dues on time. Well, this does not stop here.

Third, your CIBIL score will be dropped by 90+ points.

If you own multiple credit cards and are running out of money to settle the outstanding dues, you may get trapped in the credit card debt trap. The interest component will keep getting accumulated month on month and sooner or later you will realize that you are doomed financially.

There are ample cases where the financial life of an individual or household is completely ruined due to credit card debt and people eventually are thrown on the road. These credit card companies make it easier by allowing you to pay only **a minimum amount** per month. However, be mindful that this is again the classical trap laid by companies. The minimum amount is hardly 10 to 20% of the total outstanding balance and you are charged the high-interest rate on the remaining balance. Normally the rate of interest is 12-19%.

Then you see an offer of "One on One" movie tickets free or something else free on a new credit card. And you apply for that as well. And you end up owning multiple credit cards. Without any efforts, you get credit cards but you do not even know how to use it. Credit card companies make it easier for you by allowing you to pay only the minimum amount per month. But you never calculate that it increases the time to re-pay as well as it increases the amount of interest you pay.

Did you ever experience that your expenses went upwards after you got a credit card?

Why? Do you know it creates more psychological pain when paid in cash than a card for any purchase? When you are paying with a credit card you don't feel that you are paying because there is no immediate pinch to your pocket. And mind rests because what you have to pay is after a few days. This comes from an attitude of *"Kal ka Kal dekhenge* (कल का कल देखेंगे)*"*. And this is the biggest trap. Credit card is an entry gate for 3 traps, Debt trap, income-expenses trap, and Inflation trap.

Hence, we spend more on credit cards than we spend using cash. (But then what about the "Cashless India" suddenly you have become more patriotic.)

A credit card is used to fulfill the need for **Instant Gratification**. Your best friend is getting married and needs cash for shopping. Or it could be for an emergency purpose.

"He/she is a good friend of yours and you give your credit card to him. Afterall Friend in need is a friend indeed. He/she has promised you that they will return the amount."

There is a huge risk of ruining your relationship and it may be a start to your debt trap. The first thing is this is not legal. The other person may overuse your card or may not be able to pay back or may never return the card. (This has already happened with one of our clients.)

Most of the cases it's a never-ending loan as you keep using and keep paying it.

Very often you don't even open your credit card statement. How long do you wait to report your lost credit card? Do you make sure that you have closed your card properly? You take excessive credit limits beyond your capacity for payment. These are some of the bad habits which give you good lessons from using a credit card but in a hard way.

So, what's the way out? Should we not use the credit card altogether? Well, that will be another extreme. There always needs to be a fine balance between two extremes. By exercising proper emotional control and by being mindful of our spending habits, the cards can be made to work for our advantage. How? We shall see it in the part of the solutions.

Those who are using multiple credit cards to take undue advantage of the billing cycle consider themselves as they are smart but unfortunately, they are on the verge of a debt trap. One miss and everything collapse. So be careful.

Points to Ponder

- Credit cards are not for "Free" it's like an open loan (continuously keep using and paying it).

- Credit card is used to fulfill the need of **Instant Gratification**.

- There is a huge interest that you pay on credit cards in case of missed installment. Many bad habits associated with credit cards get you into a Trap.

CHAPTER
Seven

Home Trap

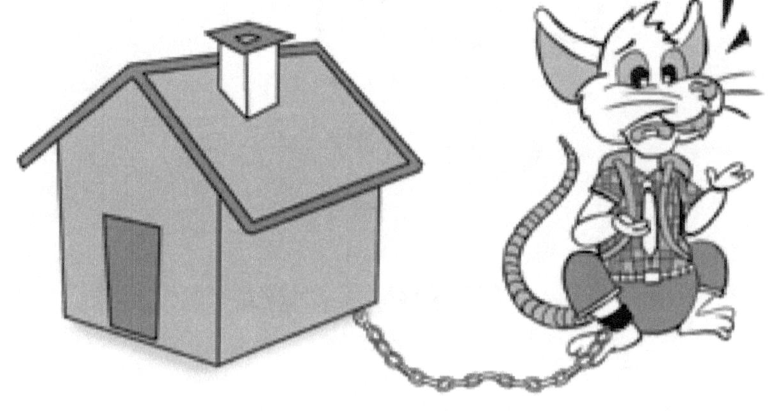

ousing loan is the most favorite loan in India and Abroad, this is normally the first loan which most investors take.

House has a very special place in heart of everyone, once child starts earning there is immediate pressure from parents for buying home, many believe that having your own property is essential to be a qualified bachelor, surprisingly these types of things happen, and on the other side many happily get married without having their own home too.

There are many stories attached to home, it's a security for someone, It's an Asset for few, it's a place to rest for few, it's a showcase for few and many more emotions, We are not against all this but we are against the wrong way which many people follow and because of these emotional decisions they create Trap for 70% of their life. Loose most earning period of life, compromise badly in life, take a lot of financial stress, can't experience what the real freedom is, what remains is just Run, Run and Run.

First, let's discuss whether there is really a need to have your own house? Or you can rent it out?

Home on Rent:

1. In India you can rent out a residential property from 0.5% to 3% (maximum without exception) of

property value, requires 6 months deposit at max. But to buy a property you have to invest 20% of the property amount as upfront + EMI almost 7% of property amount per year for the next 20 years (Considering Rate of interest for a housing loan is 9% PA and loan have taken in 80% of the cost of property).

2. What Owner expects: You to pay the rent on time and maintain property neatly.

3. There are many people in India who had taken properties to rent out. (*Famous Idiom: Fools build houses and wise Live in them.*), such people are looking for good tenants like you. (So, you have a good choice.)

4. Having a home on rent, Furniture and interior cost is avoided; you save money and invest to use it for your right goal.

5. Have the flexibility to change neighborhoods as per change in your standard of living, change in job and choice.

6. You have flexibility in relocation as you are not emotionally attached to the property.

7. No cost involved in maintaining the property.

8. As it is not your home you do not go for unnecessary furniture to showcase, so your expenses go down.

9. The agreement cost is very less. Now you can get home on long lease up to 59 months in some areas.

Home on Buy:

1. You have to pay 20% of the property value as margin Money, even you go for Loan option, so you lose the returns on this amount.

2. The stamp duty for Registration is 4% of property value, Lawyer fees and registration charges are sizable.

3. On top of that if you are going for a loan there are Loan processing + mortgage charges.

4. EMI of the property assuming you take 80% value of property loan and rate of interest is 9%, the EMI is normally 7% of the value of the property for the next 20 years

5. You have to pay maintenance charges as well as property taxes which is normally 0.8% to 1% of property value.

6. You have to do furniture as well as Interior (A nice one because you want to show off), the cost of that is normally 10%-25% value of the property.

7. You get emotionally attached to property and place and then you are closed for opportunities. (Here normally investors give a reason for children, how children can accommodate this change? but actually, children are most flexible.)

It is difficult to change home as per requirement and std. of living change.

Think on this, now a days staying on rent and as there is no assurance of children being with you, Nuclear family structure, changes in job environment, changes in social structure, moving to a good Old age home (Now many lavish old age home projects have started in India and worldwide.) is the best option financially, think on this?

Taking home is good but not at the cost of your enjoyment in life.

Part or Pre-Payment of Home loan

The second trap you get into after buying a home is whether to prepay it or part-pay the loan?

Well, we have told you so much about loan or debt and ill effects of the same. But most of you would agree that there is one loan which we can't avoid, or rather we don't want to avoid it. It is a home loan. In our opinion, there are 2 kinds of loans – Good loan and Bad loan. The loans which have potential make you RICH are Good Loans. In this loan, you really get a long-term leverage benefit. These loans come with a low-interest rate, long duration, and flexibility in payments. The assets which you create taking this loan are appreciating assets. On top of that, you get a bonus in the form of a tax break. E.g. Housing loan, Education loan.

Bad loans make your poor. It comes with a high-interest rate and short duration. Majorly these loans are taken for expenses and for depreciating assets. E.g. Personal Loan, Car Loan, Durable goods loan, Credit Card loan. Etc.

Can home loan be treated as a Good Loan? Is it a good idea to prepay the home loan? Will pre-paying a home loan can compromise your life? Let's dig a little more on this.

Basically, why would one prepay or part pay the housing Loan? The answer is to save on the interest component of the loan. However, as we will see in a short while, the pre-paying of home loans is another classical example where a common individual or household fails to understand the time value of money.

Let's say, you have recently purchased a house and have taken ₹70 Lacs home loan for 20 years @ 9% interest. Your Monthly EMI will come around ₹63,000.

Let's get down to the math behind this. On ₹70 Lac loan, the borrower will pay approximately ₹80 Lacs on interest over a period of 20 years. So, the total outflow will be ₹1.5 Cr. ₹80 Lacs is surely an immensely colossal sum and paying that much interest on ₹70 Lac loan really sounds illogical, irrational from a borrower's point of view. A borrower may consider it as dead money since it is not fetching any material value to him/her. Naturally, the instinct is to pre-pay it at the earliest to save maximum on the interest component.

However, the borrower fails to understand this interest amount on ₹80 Lacs is been paid over 20 years. Not immediate next day or month or year of taking the loan.

To put the things in a better perspective there are 2 aspects we need to understand

1. The depreciating value of Money - Try and imagine the value of those ₹80 lacs after 20 years. We are living in an emerging economy, a developing country where the inflation rate is higher compared to developed economies. In inflationary economies, the year on year rate of currency depreciation is higher. So, the value of ₹63,000 which you are paying as monthly EMI will go down with each passing year. In fact, if you do some calculations, you will find out almost 100% of your EMI amount will be your family's one-day outing expense 20 years down the line. Are we exaggerating? No.

    We assume you have a baby and we guarantee you he/she after 20 years when goes to college will ask you party contribution equal to your EMI.

    Today a family of four in metros approximately spends around ₹8000 for a one-day outing. Assuming a personal inflation rate of 11%, the same expenses 20 years down the line will be around ₹64500 which is near to your EMI even after 20 Years.

    This is how inflation erodes the value of money over time. This is how money depreciates over a period of time. So, you are going to pay to depreciate EMI against Appreciating Property.

2. The proportion of your EMI to Income will go down because your earnings will rise with each passing year. If your EMI is 40% of your monthly income as of today, it will come down to 30-25-20% over the years. So do not worry about EMI because paying today's EMI would be easy and easier for you in the future. Why you decide to **Pre-Pay Home loan?**

You decide to part pay your housing loan. What could be the reason? Are you afraid of the uncertainty of the income? Then the question is if you were skeptical about your income then why did you take a loan in the first place? So, your income which was certain becomes skeptical after taking Home Loan? Give a thought.

Another point could be that – it is painful to see the chunk of your income to go into EMI. Especially during the initial years when EMI is comprising of around 40-50% of your income.

This actually revolves around the idea that "Loan is Bad" there should not be any loan on the head, in new economy investors are still living in the past era of "Sahukari Loan" which goes on generation after generation. Come out of this old misconception!

Wakeup! You are in the new economic structure, have the Right Risk (Debt Risk) Mitigation plan in place and enjoy life!

Ok, we will leave it to you for further thinking.

As told earlier, the reason to pre-pay is to save on interest. So, if you choose this option to pre or part pay loan, how much you save on interest? 9%, right? That's the interest rate on the home loan. Since money saved is money earned, your money actually grows at the rate of around 9% which is less than your personal inflation of 11%.

Also, as you keep on pre-paying or part paying your loan, you will face a cash crunch and are exposed to Risk. You may even have to compromise your life, suppress your wishes because it requires money which you can't provide in a run of prepayment of your housing loan. So, whether your home which you had taken to become happy really brings happiness in your life or worry? It could be financially harmful in the long run. Despite doing all these juggleries it may so happen that you will eventually be able to clear all your loan only after 12-14 years. And by that time your earning will have reached a stage where you really don't need to worry about EMI.

In a nut shell-repayment of home loan, you squeeze yourself for Money, by buying your dream house but living there like a ....

Points to Ponder

- Buying Home is a professional decision or an emotional decision.

- Evaluate! Is there really a need to have your own house?

- Compare options of Home on Rent and Home on buy.

- Good Loans have the potential to make you RICH e.g. Home loan, education loan, and business loan.

- Bad loans make you POOR and they are Personal Loan, Car Loan, Durable goods loan, Credit Card loan. Etc.

- As we have learned the Time value of money in the earlier chapter while deciding about loans remember about depreciating the value of your EMI as well.

CHAPTER *Eight*

Don't Know What is Asset Class? How to Use Them?

Asset
class?

An asset class is the type of investment instruments available in the financial market (More details in the section of Behavioral Trap, *"Name is everything"*). We don't even really know which assets are available for us to invest in? What are risky assets and what are relatively safe? How to determine what asset class is suitable for a given financial goal?

You see the name, you trust the recommendation from an agent or a well-wisher, you see how many people have brought it, it's rating on various financial information sites. Is it really that important for you to know? Are you missing something? After reading till this page we are sure your answer would be 'Yes'. You are missing something more important and more crucial.

The most important thing is to know which market instrument you will be investing in, which asset class it belongs to or what is the ratio of various asset classes. Then, of course, the return, and rest all should follow. Like you can't walk by looking up in the sky you have to look down on the path.

There are 5 basic asset classes in the market where most of the financial products fit in. There are a mix and match of these asset class in most of the products. For common investors, investments don't go beyond these asset classes. Very few investors know these asset classes and fall prey to sellers in the market. Every asset class comes with specific advantages and risks. The real skill required is how to use the advantages and convert disadvantage in benefit. If you can plan this strategy then you can get freedom from Rat Race Trap.

These are the parameter on which this classification is made

1. **Risk**: When we talk about risk, we are talking about how secure, how protected the principal investment in such asset class can be?

2. **Liquidity**: How easily you can take out money from this investment. One where money can be taken out very easily, we call it as highly liquid and one where it is very difficult, we will call it as highly illiquid.

3. **Poor or Rich**: This is the possibility of a return on investment concerning inflation. In other words, the real rate of return or inflation-adjusted returns. So, if the real return is negative then such investment is making you poor, if 0 then such investment is keeping your investment value intact and if positive then such investment can make you rich.

8.1 Asset class analysis

Asset Class	Cash	Debt	Gold	Real Estate	Equity
Return	Low	Low	Medium	High	High
Risk	Low	Low	Medium	Medium	High in short term
Liquidity	High	Medium	High	Very Low	High
Poor or Rich	Poor	Poor	Poor	Rich	Rich

An investor should know the asset class where they are investing irrespective of the Name of the Product. The following are examples of different asset classes.

1. **Cash**: In Cash asset class financial instruments with high liquidity and very short maturities are considered. Such as cash in hand, Savings account, Money market Mutual funds (Liquid Funds)

2. **Debt**: FD (Fixed Deposits), RD (Recurring Deposits), all kind of post office investment options, Sukanya Samruddhi Yojana, PPF (Public Provident Fund), Traditional insurance Policies, Debt Mutual Funds, Corporate Bonds, Commercial papers, Short-term or long-term bonds, securitized products, different types of bonds..etc.

3. **Gold/ Commodity**: There are many types of commodities in the market but for the retail investor its only Gold and Silver. Beware – Any Jewelry in any form should not be considered as an asset.

4. **Real estate:** There are different types of real estate instruments like

   Residential: Flats, bungalows, plots

   Commercial: Shops, offices, shopping centers and strip malls, medical and educational buildings, hotels, Industrial Land

   Mutual Funds: Real estate investment trusts (REIT's Mutual Funds).

Real Estate was the most favorite asset class because of misunderstanding that it will never go down and can't be stolen – But now they have realized that it can be.

5. **Equity**: A stock market, equity market or share market. Equity and Equity-linked Mutual Funds,

    In the solution part, we will discuss how you can use these different asset classes for your benefit and how you can use them to get freedom from Rat Race Trap.

Points to Ponder

- Asset classes are defined on the 3 parameters of Risk, Liquidity, Poor/Rich.

- There are 5 asset classes Cash, Debit, Gold/ Commodity, Real Estate, and Equity.

- Very few investors know these asset classes and fall prey to sellers in the market.

CHAPTER
Nine

Trap of Ponzi Schemes

Quick returns.... Doubling money.... Money falling from the sky...What can be better? This is the heart of a Ponzi scheme. A Ponzi scheme uses your weakness against you. **Greed...** This is your greed to grow rich and grow rich fast. Scamsters exploit your greed. They promise you ridiculously high returns and steal your money.

A Ponzi scheme is a fraudulent investment operation that pays returns to its investors from their own money or the money paid by subsequent investors, rather than from profit earned by the individual or organization running the operation. The Ponzi scheme usually entices new investors by offering higher returns than other investments, in the form of short-term returns that are either abnormally high or unusually consistent. The perpetuation of the high returns requires an ever-increasing flow of money from new investors to keep the scheme going. (Source: References)

In short, a Ponzi Scheme is a supposed "investment" that usually does not actually buy stocks, bonds, real estate, or other common investments, but instead, takes deposits from new investors to pay returns to earlier investors. The modus operandi is simple—pay Ramesh by using the money invested by Suresh and pay Suresh by using the money invested by Paresh. It is obvious that such a scheme of paying back one investor by taking money from the other is, sooner or later, bound to fail.

One of the hallmarks of a Ponzi scheme is that it promises unusually high returns without much risk. Eventually, there are not enough funds from new investors to support the scheme, causing it to crash. But Ponzi schemes may, in fact, succeed in attracting a large number of investors before they fold up.

One of the famous Ponzi schemes was the Emu scheme of the 2012's in Erode, Tamil Nadu. Emu is a flightless bird belonging to the ostrich family. Investors were asked to make a single investment (one-time investment) say a couple of lakhs. Investors were promised multifold returns on their investment (lakhs of rupees in returns), as the Emu lays eggs for several years. These eggs are sold for over a thousand rupees. The Emu can also be sold for meat. The schemers ran away with crores of rupees leaving the emu behind. Unfortunately, Emu's eat a lot. Now, who was going to feed them? Well, not the investors at least.

I. Why do people fall prey to Ponzi Schemes?

To make it simple, let's read this funny story. There were a lot of monkeys in a village. Villagers were harassed by these monkeys. But one day a man went to this village in search of monkeys for magical medicine, which was in great demand abroad and was ready to pay handsomely.

He declared to the villagers that he would buy monkeys for ₹ 1,000/-. Villagers started roaming around to catch these monkeys. The man started buying those monkeys and when he saw inflows of monkeys is reduced he doubled the price to ₹ 2,000/-.

Looking at the doubled cost of monkeys, villagers put more effort to catch them and got a few more of them. After few days monkey flow, reduced again. Now this man doubled the price to ₹ 4,000/-. Now it was very hard to find the monkeys. Those who could find it made great money. Then this man increased the cost to ₹ 5,000/-. This way he finally increased it to ₹ 10,000/- now there were no monkeys left in the village and nearby. All monkeys were in this man's cage.

Meanwhile, the man travels back to the city for business purposes and appoints his secretary to buy a monkey and pay the money to the villagers. When the man was not around his secretary took an opportunity to make money and declared a scheme to selected people in the village. He would sell these monkeys from the cage to villagers at ₹ 5,000/- only. When the man comes back, they can sell it back to him at ₹ 10,000/- making investment double in a few days. Looking at the huge and guaranteed returns all villagers put all their hard-earned money to buy monkeys. They bought all of them. After all the monkeys were sold secretary also vanished and that man also never returned. Villagers were left with monkeys.

So why do you fall prey to Ponzi Schemes? One of the main reasons is greed. You want to make quick money in no time and throw caution to the winds. You also do not care to find out how they can afford to pay big money. A simple question you need to ask yourself. Who eats emu meat and emu eggs? Well, if no one does, then where do they get the money and how would they repay you?

Normally Ponzi schemes generally flourish when the overall investment climate is good, which makes investors think that this time it is really going to be different. Second, Ponzi schemes do offer something that many investors, high on adrenalin, can't refuse: **A high rate of return matched with consistent performance.** To add credibility to such a mouth-watering promise, Ponzi schemes may sound as if they have discovered some secret formula that is not yet publicly accessible.

Early investors of Ponzi schemes are treated like members of an exclusive club where only a lucky few can get into. This acts as an inducement for others to join. Things become merrier with an ever-increasing flow of money from new investors joining every day, which keeps the whole scheme going. But ironically, the ever-increasing number of investors brings the day of the final downfall closer. A day comes when the scheme finally evaporates into thin air.

Red flags of Ponzi scheme

There are several red flags that you can look for when you are considering whether an investment is legitimate or might be a Ponzi or other fraudulent scheme:

- High returns are promised with little or no risk
- Returns stay consistent despite market downturns
- Investments are not registered with the SEC (Securities Exchange Commission)
- The sellers are not registered with the right authority.
- Investments are not explained or kept secret
- Paperwork is kept away from investors
- Clients can't easily remove money
- Claims that the investment is available only to a select group and should not be discussed with anyone else
- High fees are charged

If you notice any of these signs when considering an investment, do more research before you commit.

II. Protecting Your Investments

Too often we leave our street smartness at the door when we think an investment or business opportunity is legitimate. When investing, keeping a wary attitude will help to protect you and your assets from those out to take your hard-earned money. If it sounds too good to be true, it probably is. Higher returns than usual indicate higher risk, up to and including the risk that the investment is a Ponzi scheme or other fraud. If you notice any of these signs when considering an investment, do more research before you commit.

Points to Ponder

- Be alert! when any investment which assures returns higher than normally available returns.

- None of the investments can give guaranteed fixed returns in a dynamic financial market.

- Assured investment is a myth.

CHAPTER
Ten

Trapped in Risks Taboo

Anything which you don't understand is unknown, uncertain or you don't care about, could be the risk. In the financial world, not understanding the various key aspects of personal finances, be it about insurance, emergency corpus or various investment avenues could be the risk. Risk is a deviation of the result as compared to your expectations. There is a great possibility that someone will take advantage of your financial illiteracy quotient and play it to their own benefit. This may permanently land you in the trap because you won't understand how your financial situation is changing. Once you know about the things which you are fearful of or increase your awareness about the same, then the Risk quotient starts going down because you will start looking to mitigate or reduce the same.

There is a lot of misunderstanding among people, what is to be considered as risk and what is now. The same is the case for investments also. The risk in investment is not the same for every investor. It varies from person to person, family to family. It in fact also varies for the same person or family depending on new situations or events that one may experience.

But there is this one thing which the majority of investors fail to understand is that there is a risk in every investment. There is hardly any investment without Risk. Few investments are considered to be safe like bank

Fixed Deposits. However, unfortunately, many banks got bankrupt across the world and many people lost thousands of crores in so-called safe fixed deposits. Some instruments are considered to be too risky but they are not that risky. With proper management and strategy, this risk can be mitigated. There are 2 types of investor some say "I don't want to take any risk "on a discussion about Equity investments, say Category 1 and there are few who say "I want to take 100% risk.", Say Category 2. These are extremes. When we reviewed the investment portfolio in detail of Category 1 client, they had already invested in a Risky asset class – They don't even know that there is no such investment available in the market (Financial Market) which is Risk-free. So unknowingly they had taken Risk which they were not aware of, it is more dangerous, it is called a blind risk. Blind Risk has a Devastating effect. The main problem with these people is they like words such as Fixed and Guaranteed (Knowing that there is no Guarantee in this Financial World), Such kind of investors chase these 2 words. Are you from this category? Then keep in mind **Enemy no.1**. when you get fixed kind of returns and also almost risk-free, then the rate of return is very less, less than inflation. Then the risk that you have here is a risk of becoming Poor day by day. Investors from the 2nd category don't know actually what is meant by taking "100% Risk". If you belong to this category then our question to you is, are you ready to lose all that money you have invested? Because when you say "100% Risk", it is both sides, either you will get a 100% return or you will lose your 100% capital. With your new understanding are you ready to take "100% Risk"? If you are, then we have the best investment option for you, where the Risk is 100% and returns can be fabulous. we know you are interested to know this. This is 100% legal. Don't get upset with an answer, face the reality there is no legal instrument available in the market but one: A game of Fortune – Lottery. Keep aside the amount which you would love to lose for 100% risk and buy tickets of the same amount, keep in mind 100% risk is gambling. So, both categories of investors' ways are not useful, then what to do, you have to strike the right balance.

Risk on investment or risk of investment

Managing financial risk is all about understating on personal finances, acquiring the right kind of knowledge, and how to use the right investment for the right purpose and tenure. When it comes to investment there are 2 factors to be considered

1. Keeping invested amount safe

2. Keeping the value of money intact.

This is where knowledge of the right investment avenues plays a key role. Because if you don't have it then there is a danger of permanently losing your hard-earned money which may never come back to you.

The value of money will remain intact only if your investment portfolio returns at least matches your inflation rate. i.e. the real rate of return is at least 0%. Even banks FD could be a risky investment because the real rate of return after adjusting for inflation and tax falls below zero. So, what is the risk in that, it is a **RISK of BECOMING POOR**. If the investment solutions you are using are making you poor then you must change them, work on your financial awareness. The investments which you think there is no risk (No risk to capital invested) there is a risk of becoming Poor. Anything which is Risk-free is Risky over a period of time. So be aware, be ready to take risks but the risk should be calculated risks and not blind risks. In the long-run inflation risk is more dangerous. Also, there is no such investment that can deliver higher returns without risk. If anyone claims so, beware that, it is a fraud or Ponzi scheme.

Change with time

One thing investor should always keep in mind is that with the passage of time, financial aspects also changes according to different aspects of your life. There may be new investment avenues that may come up or changes in the rules or regulations in existing investment vehicles may cause some impact on your financial situations. These impacts could change the financial situation in a positive or negative way. If you don't understand this and still stick to the old fashion of investments then that in itself is a rat race trap.

Always remember - as per the change you have to change.

'Change is the only constant thing in this world and if you don't change with the change then change will change you'.

—Ashish Bhave, Money & Life Freedom Coach

Social Change Risk

You had already changed many things in your life as compared to your parents, your standard of living, lifestyle, eating and drinking habits, entertainment options, choice of clothes, fashion. Everything is changed then why not Investments? Did you ever think about it?

Let's go back in time, say the late 20th century. Let's try and visualize India then. The first thing that comes to mind is the Joint Family System. This system, of the joint or extended family, was a peculiar characteristic of the Indian social life. A son after marriage won't usually separate himself from the parents but continued to stay with them under the same roof holding property and assets in common.

The family had joint property and every person has his/her share in it since the time he/she is born. The earnings of all the members were put in a common fund out of which family expenses were managed. Non-earning members had as much share as the earning members. The Indian family system was thus like a socialistic community in which **everyone earned according to his/her capacity and received according to his/her needs.**

The lifestyle was very simple. They lived as "minimalistic way", which is now back in fashion with many attractive flavors. It used to be *'SadhaAachar, UchchaVichar'*. Lesser expenses, fewer demands; fewer needs, less stress, etc. They were the hard worker, always busy with something. Be it a farmer or a person working for some company or organization. A person once got employed will stick to it for his/her entire working life span. Honesty and Loyalty to the firm were common characteristics then. Of course, there was high job security too.

Though they had less income, managing the house was still easy because they had someone to count on in the joint family.

India in the past:

| Large families | Long work-span | High job security |

So according to their lifestyle, they never had to worry about these following things

1. Retirement planning: They did not have to worry about planning for their retirement because they knew that my bigger family will take care of them. (Earlier there was a possibility: If not the 1st kid then the 3rd one will take care. If not the 3rd then 7th one will surely look after them.) Generation after generation they used to stay at the same place, same house and all the resources were shared. The person working for government departments used to get a lifelong pension for themselves and the spouse.

2. Job insecurity: No need to update or upgrade self, no stress of not having a job tomorrow, no worry of not being able to pay their loan as losing a job was a very rare thing.

3. Emergency fund: Having a large family at times of emergency is like a boon. All come in together to help the one out of the crisis, so they never felt the need to have an emergency fund with them.

4. Lifestyle: Having said earlier they had a very quiet lifestyle, so even if income stopped or they got retired early, they did not need much. The best options for them used to be to do God's Bhakti and visit a pilgrimage and look after the grandsons during their sunset years.

5. No Loans: As requirements were less and staying in an ancestral home there was no need for a home loan or a personal loan. So, there were no liabilities due to loans.

India Today

During the last quarter of the century, there has been a radical change in the social fabric of our country. There has been a gradual disintegration of the joint family system and the emergence of a 'nuclear family'. Reflecting on the rise of the nuclear families in urban India, these households are small in size more than 80 percent have three to four members with no senior citizens and less than 20 percent have more than two children.

Slowly we had forgotten about the *Saral Jeevan* lifestyle and got trapped in all kinds of materialistic things. Less is not enough anymore. Actually, even more, it is not enough now for many of us. Because of the computer revolution, the speed of change is multifold and thus expectations. In this growing world of expectations, peer pressure and competition, our job is less secure. Keep performing is the Mantra of companies. Companies are always on the lookout for cost optimization and how more can be achieved with less either through the automation and/or by trimming the workforce. Cruel and unrealistic deadlines, late-night working and slogging, availability over weekends and late nights even on vacations is slowly becoming a norm.

On the other hand, people are looking for less working span and many want to retire early. Working all life is no more a passion. Long working hours and continued stress have negative health implications. Constantly evolving technology demands that an individual has to keep him/her updated with the latest trends and technologies all the time to keep himself /herself employable. Government jobs are reducing. The luxury of lifelong pension after retirement is gone.

An increase in stress level, increased demands at the personal, family, social and work level, more wants more expenses, and small family makes it more difficult to manage. The heightened stress is giving rise to lifestyle diseases at an earlier age. The medical advances have ensured an increased life span for an individual. The more you live, the more you need the money.

And we make it more difficult by doing the same old typical invest and savings as our ancestors did, forgetting that their needs and wants plus lifestyle was different than ours. They did not need retirement planning, but we do. We don't have 7 or 8 children now, maybe just 1 or 2 who themselves find it difficult to live their own life. How will they take care of us? And in the nuclear family fabric, the children will soon start living separate and independent life the moment they start earning and are financially independent.

Plus, a high level of job insecurity adds to the situation like putting more oil in the fire. We need to be ready with any kind of emergency in case of job loss. Sadly, we are not really doing any such planning, we come under the influence of our elders and follow all that they did, which does not really come to our help at the time of need.

Shorter work-span

Lower job security

Smaller families

So, we need to change our minds, open our thoughts and look around for new doors by walking on the new road /path.

Risk of losing income generation capability

Apart from this many investors are ignoring the biggest Risk of Life, its life itself.

If there are financial dependents on you or in another way if there is any financial liability on you, then you have to have a proper protection system for the same. Yes, I am talking about Insurance cover.

Are you a responsible husband? a Responsible mother? a Responsible Father? A Responsible Son or daughter (Where parents are financially dependent on you)? if yes, then have you protected your financial liability? Unfortunately, most of the times the answer is no!? Even if you are well educated.

Face the reality, an unfortunate event can happen with you also, not only with the person next door. Don't just tell your family that you love them, prove it!

Most of the time there is a problem, under Insurance.

In the coming section, we will understand how and which path we should walk on to enjoy our life the way we want.

Points to Ponder:

- Every investment has risk associated with it.
- There is some risk that is visible and you are aware of it and if you think that there is no risk in the specific investment then there is a great possibility that you are taking a blind risk.
- The time has changed and now you have to change your investment philosophy.

CHAPTER
Eleven

Putting the Cart Before Horse

Do you put cart before the horse? I am sure you would say this is a foolish question. Who insane person would do that? But don't you really do this?

We normally ask our clients these 3 questions:

1. Where have you invested money till date?

2. Why have you invested?

3. What are you expecting from the investment?

Last 2 questions seem to be a little confusing, isn't It?

Most investor's answer for question 2 would be like: I invested because a friend told me about it, or relative, my husband, or Bank relationship manager suggested. Some might say I read in the newspaper, heard from a News channel. Some just say I have a gut feeling about this. And when one does not know why one has invested, it is not surprising that answer to the 3rd question most of the time is "I Don't know", "I am not sure". This is absolutely ridiculous.

What are your answers? Same? If yes, take a pause and think, introspect.

There are so many efforts you are putting to earn the money, many times at the cost of personal or family commitments and when the time comes to use that hard-earned money judiciously, you say I don't know for what purpose I invested and what returns to expect? If you don't know how to make your money equally work the way you work, then what's the point in putting those long hours, slogging, making personal sacrifices, putting family commitments on back priority, missing your child's performance on an annual day?

Actually, before investing, you should know why you are investing. But here you don't even care thinking about it. Mostly, we blindly depend on the so-called expert (Mostly on Free advice from a friend, parent, neighbor, colleague, boss, watercooler side/coffee machine side adviser or someone who wants to sell you something for His/her benefit). No wonder people either suffer a loss or gain below-average returns on their investment because the purpose itself is missing.

That is how many people live by doing the last thing first and hoping to get the desired outcome. Some people like to follow the herd, does not matter even if they are going to commit some crime or going to jump off the hill, they just want to be a part of the herd and don't want to be left alone or behind.

They actually do things without a purpose, and when it's done without a reason or done for no reason, in particular, it might never help you when you need it.

There are many financial instruments in the market which are designed for a different duration if you could not use them for the right duration, for the right purpose, there is a great possibility of losing money.

When you plan for your vacation what is the first thing that you decide? Destination? or Vehicle? First, you decide on destination then based on the destination you choose a vehicle i.e. Flight, Train, Car or cycle. In the same manner, you must follow below 3 steps:

1. Decide the financial goal,

2. Its duration,

3. Investment vehicle for the same.

Rather than choosing a vehicle first and then deciding the goal of mapping it with a goal. **Before investing you should know why you are investing.**

Points to Ponder

- Before investing decide the purpose of investment.

- Follow 3 steps process for investing. Decide goal, know the duration and select the right investment vehicle.

- It's more important to make enough money available at the time when you need it.

CHAPTER *Twelve*

Taking Your Best Friend for Granted

ON TIME
DELAYED
LATE
?

We all have that one person in our life whom we always wish to stand by our side, help us in all kind of situations, and does not interfere in our life till we ask them to.

They won't ever come to us; we need to approach them first and then just trust them and forget the rest. But we always take such a person for granted. We think we can go to them at the last minute and they should be ready to help us by doing some miracle or magic. Unfortunately, it does not work that way. They don't hold a magic wand that will provide readymade solutions for any kind of problem, however simple or complex the problem may be. In reality, they also need time, to understand our needs, situations to help us.

Remember, how in Mahabharata, Krishna was one of the main reasons for Pandava's victory. He was alone enough to help them win the battle with his strategy. But to have Krishna on their side, Arjun had to go to him and wait patiently for him to wake up and listen to him. And when he was on their side, all they had to do was to be patient, and believe in Krishna.

In the same way, as Pandavas, had Krishna as their best friend, we have a best friend too when it comes to investing. And this friend has similar traits to Lord Krishna.

Firstly, you need to approach him to come and help you win the battle and get financial freedom.

Secondly, once he comes on your side just trust him and wait patiently

Thirdly, like Lord Krishna, he too is alone enough for us to win the battle provided we give him time to prepare for the war. We call him, **'Lord compounding'**.

Wondering why we called him Lord? Its because he works according to the important laws of nature, 'law of multiplication, the law of abundance and law of giving & taking'.

No wonder Worlds Respected Scientist Albert Einstein honored the **Lord Compounding**as '8th Wonder of the World'.

For example, You invest Rs 10 lakh (give) wait for the next 10 years (patience) and then you get (take) around Rs 40 lakh (multiplied and in abundance) (Considering ROI @14.5% PA for 10 years)

If you observe in nature you could relate Compounding effect with Tree. You know the tree is a creation of a single seed and it creates millions of seeds every year once grown.

But we don't let him do his work well, because we either invest late or are in a hurry to take out the investments soon. And as he can't go against his rules, he can't deliver the best results or returns to us and we start to disbelieve him.

Do you know all Financial Problems are like asymptomatic diseases that show indications when more than 70% damage is already done? For such diseases most of the time solution available is Surgery? But another solution is prevention. They say *A stitch in time saves nine.*

Do you know when we invest; we get returns in 2 different ways.

1. **Simple** – Your principal remains the same throughout and profit (or interest) on that would separate, at the end of tenure the total of the amount is given to you. (In all traditional insurance policy calculation of Bonus on your sum assured (life cover) is done in this manner, Bonus on your insurance policy is a Profit share.)

2. **Compounding** - In compounding, principal grows every time, when there is a profit (or interest) it gets added in the principal amount and this increased principal generates profit in next year thus the returns grow fast.

Future value with Simple interest is calculated as –

P + (P*R*N).

And

Future value withCompounding interest is calculated as –

P * (1+R) ^N

Where

P: Principal amount invested

R: Rate of Interest

N: No. of years of investment

Just to understand if you invest ₹ 100 with 10% interest per year for 25 years - with Simple interest, you will get ₹ 350 as maturity amount and ₹ 1083.47 from compounding interest, higher the duration higher the gap between returns.

As tree requires time to grow and give fruits same with Compounding. You will get the fantastic benefit if you give enough time and this is where the most investor fails. They want immediate returns.

See this table if you invest ₹1,00,000 how much you can get if the returns are 10% yearly.

Years invested	Amount (₹)
5	1,61,051
10	2,59,374
15	4,17,725
20	6,72,750
25	10,83,471
30	17,44,940

See the benefits; you get returns in multiples with increased time.

In compounding even, a small change in the rate of return can make significant change in maturity value. In above table we saw the returns with 10% now let's see the returns with 12%. Just increase by 2% gives a great difference.

Years invested	Amount (₹)
5	1,76,234
10	3,10,585
15	5,47,357
20	9,64,629
25	17,00,006
30	29,95,992

In the 3rd part of the book we will delve more on how you can use **Lord compounding** to your advantage. We will see the mathematical calculation of the power of compounding and how to use it in our favor to win the battle of becoming financially free and beat our major enemy 'Inflation'.

Points to Ponder

- Always invest in an instrument where you get Compounding rate on your investment and not the simple.

- Before investing know what is compounding rate of return of your investment. A small change in Rate of return can create a great difference in the long term.

- As you give enough time to grow a tree and regularly water it, let your investbents grow for a longer time along with a regular review.

CHAPTER
Thirteen

Trap of Low Liquidity

There are people in the society who keep very minimal cash or balance in their savings accounts and invest the rest in such a way that the money gets locked. These people have a phobia of spending the money. These are mostly the people who are unable to identify their needs and wants. They are completely unaware of the financial goals in their life and the money that is needed to fulfill those goals. This ignorance does not enable them to decide on how much money they should keep, how much they should invest, and how much they should spend.

So, they adopt a strategy called – Low Liquidity – to keep their expenses at a minimum. Apart from whatever is needed to fund their basic day to day operational expenses, they invest everything. They invest everything that they can. The problem with this strategy is that investment mostly happens in wrong avenues since the objective is locking money and hence absolutely not in a position to choose the right investment vehicle.

Have you seen friends who never carries his/her wallet along with them? Or do you have an uncle/aunty who always needs to borrow from you because their strategy is not to keep any amount with them as cash or in a saving account? They do eventually return you your money in some time but they don't have money when it's needed.

Buying an unaffordable, bigger house (assuming that I can buy a house once in a life) at the beginning of the career is another common cause of low liquidity. Purchasing the house is a dream for anybody and everybody. It gives a sense of achievement (albeit at the cost of many more compromises and strains for subsequent 10 to 15 years). People tend to overspend while purchasing the house and do stretch their budget and wallets to the extreme. With significant pie of the income going for home loan EMI, there is little money left to spend.

We also have people who love spending. For them enjoying today is the most important thing. They never think about their future responsibility. These people live like they are born to spend. The result is a money crisis and no liquidity, once the money is over. These kinds of people get into a credit card trap which leads to a bigger debt trap.

Do you know people in business (doesn't matter if it's small or big) ask you money? Did you ever wonder how come a person running a business has to borrow money from you? People in business tend to invest in everything. If they don't keep an accounting of how the rupee is earned and how it is spent, they will always be short of funding their operational expenses.

These kinds of people are dependent and confident in their friends and relatives for help in emergencies but they don't know that their friends and relatives are also thinking in the same way.

These were some samples where people do not keep enough cash with them. Beware of such people around you. Lending such people beyond a reasonable limit can create a lot of stress in your family life and also there is a high chance that they may dig a deeper hole in your finances.

I. Impact of Low Liquidity during Financial Emergency

We cannot predict situations such as job loss or an illness or an accident. These are unfortunate events where our earning is temporarily stopped since we are unable to perform our professional duties. In case of a medical emergency, the maximum expenses occur in the first 72 hours of an emergency. During such times we must have enough money to fulfill the expenses. **We should have money either in saving accounts or liquid funds that can be withdrawn and made available in a couple of hours. This is called an emergency corpus and is a must-have for every household.**

If you have not maintained the emergency corpus then the only option left is to borrow from someone or dig into the investments like equities or Mutual Funds or real estate. God forbid but if the equity market is going through the depression, then one may have to sell their shares or Mutual Funds at losses to make up for the emergency corpus.

If one is invested in illiquid assets such as Real estate then it's very difficult to liquidate them in a shorter period of time. Selling real estate assets such as land, plot or apartment can take anything between 3 months to 2 years. In such a situation one may be forced to sell at a ridiculously discounted price because they have lost the power of negotiating.

Taking Personal loans, loans on credit cards has a nasty potential to completely derail one's financial life because of the interest on loan trap you get into. The Credit card interest can be as high as 50% annually and there are cases where people have gone bankrupt to settle the dues.

II. Identifying a Real Financial Emergency

So now we understand that there is something called emergency corpus. Let's say we have parked some random amount there. The next biggest challenge is to spend this money only on a real emergency. Having an amount that is instantly available for spending can be very tempting. And if the due diligence is not applied then in no time that money can disappear.

Do we know what emergency is? There is a wedding in the family and we need to do the shopping. Is this an emergency? Your friend asked you for some money urgently. Is this an emergency? Your fridge is not big enough to stuff all the material that you have purchased today. It's your wife's or girlfriend's birthday or your marriage anniversary and you want to pamper by purchasing that amazing necklace to her. Is this an emergency?

All these may look like an emergency. But those are not. Those can wait. You can purchase that expensive necklace for your wife or girlfriend 6 months down the line. You can curtail your wedding shopping and purchase what is really needed.

After using the emergency funds for real emergencies, you need to make sure that you refill it. Because again any other real emergency can strike any moment and we have already explained the effects of not having an emergency corpus. As mentioned in the start, real emergencies can be a job loss, major accidents, medical emergencies, natural calamities, etc.

Having a sufficient emergency fund provides you that much needed financial cushion and will safeguard you from falling into the trap of high-interest credit card debt or personal loans. A better financial cushion also gives us the strength to handle the emergency in much-composed way since we are in a better position to think rationally.

Points to Ponder

- Low liquidity can get you into a trap by not having money when you need it which leads to borrowing at high interest rates.

- Urgent need of money snatches your negotiating power.

- Emergency funds should be used only after identifying that it's a real financial emergency.

CHAPTER
Fourteen

Don't Understand Risk and Types of Risk

Once I was flying to Delhi for vacation. While standing in the queue to collect boarding pass I started observing the people around me.

1. A gentleman in his fifties was carrying a suitcase with 2 locks, the technological in-built lock (luggage lock) and a normal lock (padlocks).

2. I also saw this young lady with the biggest suitcase I had ever seen and that too was unlocked even though there was an in-built lock.

3. Most of the passengers though had ensured that they have locked their baggage.

This gentleman (with 2 locks for his baggage) especially made me curious and I started thinking what could be the reason for using 2 locks? Is he feeling too insecure or unsafe? To water my thirst for curiosity I went and had a small talk with him.

The man said he does not trust modern technology, and can't rely on it, so he is using a traditional lock over and above inbuilt one. I inquired if he had taken travel insurance or had term and Accidental Death and Disability (ADDB) cover in place, as his life is also at risk because of traveling. He said he does not have travel insurance but few traditional insurance plans.

Next going to the lady, she replied saying, what will be taken away? And if anything is stolen, I shall complain against the airport authority. For insurance, she said she does not need any as she is fit and fine.

While talking to this lady the couple that was just standing behind me in the queue also joined the conversation. When I asked the husband about the insurance he affirmatively replied as Yes. **I cover the risk of my death first and then the belongings.**

The gentleman inspired me by his words. This provoked me to think as to what's the risk (both life and financial), how to avoid or minimize it? What can happen if the risk really materializes?

We all know that death is certain but the time of death is uncertain. And hence it could be the biggest risk in our life. The risk is the possibility of losing something of value. The untimely death of a breadwinner could mean a financial disaster for his family.

It is so rightly said that when you are thinking about or searching for something, you may find such examples very nearby to you. Let us quote a couple of examples that will give an understanding of the financial risks arising out of life's uncertainties.

- A middle-aged person living in our society and working in big MNC drawing handsome salary and at senior management designation died all of a sudden because of heart attack. He was survived by a wife and a 15-year-old daughter. He was the only bread earner of the family. This was obviously a shocker to all of us who were his neighbours.

- Few days later with one of our client's reference his widow approached me with the financial documents that he had left behind to see how much of wealth he has left and if there is any insurance? Unfortunately, as it happens, he had only couple of traditional insurance plans that could fetch his family a sum of 10 to 15 lacs apart from some stocks and fixed deposits. Looking at their lifestyle this was too little for them and wife who had been a home maker till now had to start working in order to survive.

- One of my cousins who is a doctor and has seen many such cases where patients don't have enough money to even stay in the hospital or get their treatment done well. She shared a story of a patient she really appreciated. A working lady had met with an accident and was paralyzed below her waist, which meant she cannot walk, get up, or move on her own. Being a working woman, her income had come to halt, sadly the expenses would not halt though.

- But she was financially sorted. She had an Accidental Death and Disability Plan (ADDB) and also health insurance. ADDB ensured that she got a regular weekly payment owing to her temporary disability whereas health insurance covered her hospitalization expenses. Well, the physical and emotional trauma that she would have undergone is irrecoverable but at least adequate insurance cover ensured that she gets well treatment and does not have to worry about the day to day life and expenses.

- From these cases, it was clear to me that you need to have the right insurance to cover for financial risks. How to decide the right amount, we shall see that in the next section.

- The above was an experience that one of our Co Author had been through.

Points to Ponder

- The bread winner in the family is the most valuable asset for family.

- As a human being you are exposed to risks. It is always better to have a risk mitigation plan in place.

- Emotional losses cannot be but financial losses can be covered.

CHAPTER
Fifteen

Behavioral and Emotional Traps

Behavioral biases are irrational beliefs or behaviors that can unconsciously influence our decision-making process. Let us discuss a couple of them here.

15.1 Mental Calculations

Consider you are in a book shop and want to buy a book which is costing Rs 500. When you are about to buy a book one person tells you that if you go to the next shop which is just 500 meters from here you will get the same book at a 30% discount. What will you do?

In another scenario, you are at a car dealer and want to purchase a brand-new car costing Rs. 10 lacs. When you are about to take the final decision, you get a piece of information that the same car is costing 1% less in another dealer who is just 500 meters away. Now, what you will do?

Research says most people will prefer to go to another outlet in the first scenario but not that much interested in second. Surprisingly this happens because of mental calculations. This calculation is done on the basis of percentage and not in amounts. In the first scenario, its 30% while in the second scenario is just 1%. But the amount wise first case is Rs. 150 and the second scenario its Rs. 1000.

15.2 Equity Investors trapped in Emotions of Fear & Greed

The lure of big money always draws investors towards the stock markets. Pick any given 10-year time frame for the NIFTY or Sensex (India's benchmark stock market index), and you are likely to discover that the index has grown between 12% and 15% (compound annualized) during that period. Similarly, top-ranked Equity Mutual Fund Investments also boasts of impressive returns over longer time frames – when it comes to long term investments.

Ironically, despite this impressive track record, it is not uncommon to find that at least 8 out of 10 retail investors end up losing money in the market. One of the very common reasons for the same is that equity still is been perceived as a speculative instrument, something like gambling where people think that they can make big money overnight. They do get swayed by emotions of fear and greed and blindly follow the herd and ultimately end up losing the money. Let's study this in a bit more detail –Buying Due to Greed or Euphoria

This would surely rank as the number one reason why retail investors lose money in the Equity market. Most institutional investors (the ones who make money in the long run) scout for buying opportunities ("bottom-fishing") after markets have fallen considerably. That's probably why they end up reaping rewards from the markets. On the other hand, the unaware retail investor always rushes in to buy stocks after they've already escalated dramatically. The key driver behind this unfortunate phenomenon is greed or euphoria, which clouds rational judgment.

Selling Out Due to Hype and Fear

Euphoria's evil twin is fear. The retail investors buy high and sell low. They get hooked to someone on TV who starts making doomsday predictions – most likely AFTER the markets have already dropped considerably.

There is this famous quote from legendary Warren Buffett – '*We simply attempt to be fearful when others are greedy and to be greedy only when others are fearful.*'

Churning & Burning

Equity investing success is synonymous with patience. Always remember the law of the farm.

The concept behind the Law of the Farm is simple: A farmer cannot expect to reap a bumper crop by being lazy for three months and then "cramming" to catch up. Similarly, the greatest successes in life are built slowly and deliberately through focused, consistent, high-quality efforts on a daily basis.

Once you've done your research, analyzed and shortlisted and bought your stocks, be sure not to churn them in a hurry. Moving in and out of Equity because 'there's a better opportunity available' or 'there's a new fund on offer' isn't a wise strategy. It's best to hold on to good Stocks or Equity Mutual Funds for the long term.

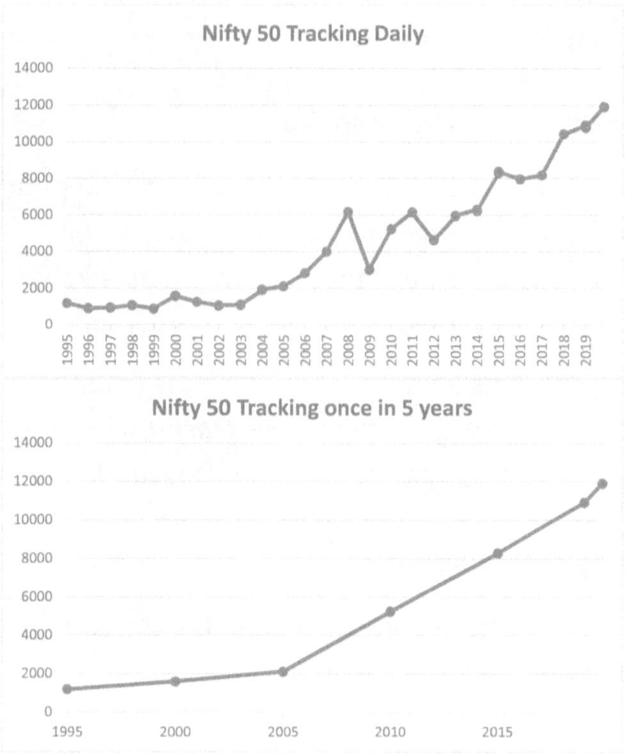

Impatience

Markets will not move according to your whims and desires. In fact, there may be extended periods of time that prices will stay depressed in spite of the overall economy improving. Once again, if you have conviction in the story of the business and investment decisions, exercise patience. You don't want to exit in a hurry and watch the same stock race ahead after you exit.

Checking Stock Prices Obsessively

Whatever you do, do NOT check your stock portfolio obsessively! There are people who are continuously monitoring the stock ticker either on TV or Mobile. Obsessively checking prices will surely lead to losses in your portfolio, as you'll literally be inviting a host of behavioral biases to push you into making irrational investment decisions. How often do you check your pulse or heart rate? Do you check it every 10 minutes, an hour? The answer is obviously 'No'. If anyone is doing that then he or she surely is going to witness an unstable emotional as well as mental behavior. Checking the stock prices obsessively is no different. Stock prices are moving up and down every second. Watching your portfolio moving up or down will surely make you lose your peace of mind.

Becoming Rich Overnight Syndrome

People with strong desire to get rich quickly; resort to lot of risky instruments. Gambling is one of them. The derivatives trading in equity markets also called as future and options is another one. It is a sure shot way of becoming poor, and also to lose mental peace and calm.

"In Investing always remember that Rome was not built in a DAY."

"In TRADING always remember that Hiroshima and Nagasaki were destroyed in a DAY..."

Guru Warren Buffett has termed derivative trading as a weapon of mass destruction. There is another famous quote – *'Those who do not remember the history are condemned to repeat it – George Santayana'*

In a bull market scenario, each and every stock starts scaling new highs with each passing day. As usually happens -with so much euphoria around the stock market- traders (not investors!) start feeling that it is the place to make easy money. The words and acts like sense, rational and wisdom are been treated as backward and naïve.

Media, analysts, brokerage houses start talking about the stocks that traders can take the position and make quick money. Brokerage houses come up with fancy plans to lure people so that more and more people start trading into derivatives (& ultimately brokers earn more commission from increased participation). One started hearing stories about some neighbors, some friends who made fortunes using derivatives and so on.

With the almost one-way direction in the market, derivative participants do get some initial success by earning some profit. This inducts a false sense of confidence among them and leads them to take higher risks than they can afford. They take loans at much higher interest rates. They dip into the savings that are meant for their goals. They start feeling that he or she is unique and has cracked the magic formula to earn profits and become rich overnight which no one previously has been able to do.

And then one fine day market starts correcting. The position that they have taken starts bleeding and they end up in big losses. Whatever the small gains that are made previously are wiped out and they are left with a deeper and bigger cut.

There are few examples where they have lost fortunes and have become forever poor in the 2008 stock market crash. There were many investors working in one of the Top 5 IT companies in India, at a very senior position and have made a lot of money when IT was a sunrise industry and booming. This has happened with one of the colleague of our co-author. He quit the job and become a full-time stock investor. That's not too bad, we will say. Investing in the stock market can be a full-time profession and many wizards have made a fortune out of it.

This friend of ours had his chance of luck and saw initial success for a couple of years and as usually happens with most of the human beings — he let the success go to his head. He thought he had become the stock market wizard. Started trading in derivatives. Took loans, leveraged high margins and one day he lost. He lost so badly that he had to sell his house to service the loan obligations. He went into depressions and his entire financial life was derailed.

Guru Buffett said it long time back.

There should be only 2 rules to be followed in stock market.

Rule No.1: Never lose money.

Rule No.2: Never forget rule No.1

15.3 Trap of 'Free'

The beauty is that people are ready to pay for "Free" things without thinking and this is the biggest trap. The "buy one gets one free" offer result in a person purchasing the items that he/she does not need at all. These unplanned expenses can create a big hole in your pocket. Carefully look at your wardrobe or storeroom and you will find how much junk you have created in your life by falling prey to 'Free' trap and purchasing the useless stuff.

One needs to understand the hidden charge behind the word free. As they say "there are no free lunches". Everything has some value attached to it, monetary, or non-monetary. For e.g. You hear about the gift voucher worth ₹ 500. Most of the time it will come with some terms and conditions. Like Voucher Validity is only for a certain duration of time and in order to avail the voucher benefit you need to make some mandatory purchase, say ₹ 5000. What's the end result? Are you feeling great that you have saved ₹500? Yes? Well, that's precisely is the problem. You have been completely fooled. This is a classic example of पैसे में कमाया रुपये में गवाया.

A shop owner has made a profit on the sale of ₹5000. You ended up losing ₹5000 because you want to get the benefit of that ₹500. There is a great possibility that you might purchase things which you do not want. So, a gift voucher of ₹500 is a bait for your ₹4500.

Please understand that the merchants are not there for charity or to offer you free lunches.

Many times, free cost us more expensive. You might have heard of opportunity cost, which means we lose the opportunity of one thing because we selected the other thing over the former thing.

For example, there is a wonderful fridge available at a huge discount and some free accessories. You are in need of a new fridge but not really on an urgent basis. But you think the product is good and giving a great offer, so why not buy it now? After buying you come to know that the production for this is closed and a new high-tech fridge is been launched with a launch offer too. Now if your fridge has some problem or would need any part changed it won't be easily available and you may have to bear extra cost for it.

So here you lost the opportunity cost of buying a new high-tech fridge because you thought the one with discount and free accessories was a better product.

The same happens to us when it comes to investing. We look for people or channels where we can get free advice, like news channels, social media posts, neighbors, relatives, friends, and agents. We ask, e.g., about the home loan to an insurance agent. Basically, we consult all those people who have zero expertise in financial planning or investing.

Free is also used in financial consultancy when you have a good amount of money in your bank account. You get a call from Bank that they have assigned relationship manager for you and this relationship manager will help you in managing all your financial goals and needs. And yes, the services are absolutely free. "Free" is the word that attracts people and without thinking much people fix the appointments with such relationship managers. Here what they fail to understand is that the so-called relationship manager (RM) is not your RM but they are bank's RMs. They are interested in getting more business for the bank so that they can earn more commissions or get promotions & increments. Your financial interests are least important to them. They will try to sell you the products that fetch maximum margin for the bank and hence more lucrative commission for them. But since people are fascinated with "Free", they fall prey for such relationship managers and buy many investment products which they don't understand and also are not fit for their financial purpose. What and why does this word attract us so much? Without thinking we fall for it just to realize later that we are fooled. Beware, Free is a trap that is difficult to get out from but way easy to get into.

Do we do this with our health too? If you have an eye irritation would you go to an ortho specialist or an eye specialist? Or if you got a skin allergy would you go a gynaecologist or a dermatologist? Sounds silly and stupid question, right? We, of course, go to the expert doctors of that field then why not, when it comes to wealth? We do have wealth doctors available but still, we don't go and pay fees there. We chose to take free advice which cost us more than the charge of wealth doctor, plus the time that is lost which is completely irrecoverable. Without thinking much we all go for free things. We are not saying all free things are bad, some are genuinely good deals. But you need to be smart to know which is a good deal and which is bad.

15.4 Name is everything

The world-renowned English poet William Shakespeare said: "What is in the name?"

We think he might not have invested money, otherwise, he would not have dared to say this.

For most of the investor, the name is everything. People invest in an investment instrument that has an attractive name. And that's why many of the products have a very attractive name and few of them also come with limited time offer (to add more attraction).

People just fall prey to all the fancy and creative names given to the product or the scheme and forget to get into the details of the product. They have developed a belief system that products with creative and attractive names surely will be of good quality and a great product. But does it really mean that way?

Let us try to guess some investment instrument from their name

Enjoy Golden years, Smart Star, Dream Car, Dream home, Sweet home, Proud parent, Millionaire / Billionaire plan, Gain more, Happy wedding, Seedha Jeevan.

Surely these types of few names look attractive and investor invests without much thinking. But when you really study the objective of these instruments, you will really get confused. Whether this product is thinking about the investor's goals or Mediator's goals? Whose child will be smart yours or Mediators? Who is going to enjoy Golden years YOU OR ......?

Most of the investors invest in name with emotional calling without knowing what it is? Strange but true. An investor takes a lot of effort to earn. He/she will fight for every rupee till it gets into his/her pocket. Once it is in the pocket the value goes down drastically. People do get caught in the name trap when the decisions are taken with Emotions and not with Brain.

Normally we have observed people-" *EARN Money to become Rich and Invest to become POOR*" and if you are one of them then you are already in RRT.

What will you do if you have to buy a new Mobile? You will search on the net or visit a couple of mobile shops. You will try to understand what features it offers? You will compare the price, display, size, battery life, camera, memory, etc. Once you zero on a particular piece, you will try and find the shop or website that is giving you the best price. Don't you do all these things? You do this all for things which are not as important as your life.

Unfortunately, when it comes to investments exactly reverse happens. You are reluctant to take an informed decision (sometimes with a lame excuse that- investments are too complex to understand) about investments which are actually one of the key aspects of life. Your future, your retirement, your child's education goals depend on it. This decision is taken with trust mostly on unknown people. This trust is not a calculated Risk but a blind Risk. With trust, the responsibility is given to someone else but here most investors fail to understand that if that person breaches the trust, not he/she but you are going to suffer the most.

15.5 Guaranteed returns

What can you say for sure? Like, guarantee that the thing will happen the way it was promised to occur? We all know that death and taxes are certain to happen but how it will happen we don't know that.

Remember those advertisements on television about some products which guarantee the result and we bought them. In reality, that product will most of the time turn out to be a waste of money because it gave results maybe just 10-20 or 30 % of what was guaranteed. Because **guarantee is always conditional.**

Like the slim belt? How they show the before and after picture of a person who used the belt! I always feel that those are two different individuals and we have been fooled by smart digital technology. Or even the fairness cream ads. Many of these brands are easily convincing us that it will work wonders and we will get guaranteed results in quick or no time without to have to put in too much effort or hard work. But in reality, they are smart in fooling us. The words like guaranteed are the trick. It so also happens that at times we are skeptical and have a kind of sense that there could be something fishy. Yet we all fall prey to such things because we get obsessed with the term 'Guarantee'.

The companies and the advertising agencies that promote the brands do have an in-depth understanding of how human psychology works. What appeals to an individual, to a male, a female or a kid? They smartly exploit these psychological tricks in their favor and we get trapped into those. The words like Guaranteed, Free, Buy one Get One Free, Free Sale up to 50% discount, Sale 50%+50% discount directly appeals that aspect of the brain or human psychology that is craving for some instant gratification.

No wonder financial agents do use these tricks and people fall in for such schemes where guaranteed returns are offered, and then lose the money or lose its value. The schemes or investments that are directly linked to the markets like Stocks, Mutual Funds, Bonds and Debt

Funds, Real Estate, etc. are a function of multiple factors that can influence the end returns. No one can predict that. No one can assure that. No returns are guaranteed. If anyone is giving you the assurance of returns then for sure there is some gimmick and it is guaranteed that you are getting into a trap.

Points to Ponder

- When it comes to management of money professional approach is important. With emotional approach most of the times you may find yourself in a trap.

- There are 2 emotions which interferes in your decision making. Fear and Greed.

- When it comes to investment find out, how useful is it for you and not because the name is attractive.

- Keep this in mind and act accordingly as, there are no Free lunches in the world. Most of the "Free" things will turn out to be costly for you.

- Stay away from any investment where you are assured about the returns from the investment.

CHAPTER
Sixteen

Other Traps

riends, there are many such traps in the market. We tried and covered some significant ones. If you have fallen prey to any one or more of these traps, then you surely are becoming poorer with each day gone by. Your quest to become rich is actually leaving you poor.

Who has created all these traps? Of course, you only. Thanks to your financial illiteracy, negligence, and laziness on your part to develop your financial IQ.

Unfortunately, in our education system, no one tells you about how to manage your money (There are many things which are not taught in schools or colleges but you still acquired them, think). So even if you are academically educated, when it comes to your money management, financial management, you are illiterate.

The good part is you have started making yourself financially educated. You have come so far, and that tells your willingness to come out of the RRT. Continue reading through the remainder of the book where we try and present some practical, easy to implement steps.

If you are able to follow & implement all that we will be discussing from now on, you take a very firm position to get freedom from Rat Race Trap. You will increase your chances to get financial freedom in the near future.

So, without asking you to hold on curiosity any more, we are happy to introduce you to the beautiful, simple, interesting, implementable and easy to understand solutions to get freedom from RRT and start your journey to get Rich & Happy in life.

The Way Ahead:

We hope that now you are able to identify areas that you need to work on and the traps that you are into with the help of the list that you had started after the first section. Now in the next section, you will get ideas about how to free yourself from these traps. After the next section, you are requested to create your own strategy to get Freedom from Rat Race Trap.

PART
Three

Freedom from Rat Race Trap (RRT)

Freedom to live life the way you want.

Freedom from all financial responsibilities.

Freedom from all financial liabilities.

Freedom to pursue a dream lifestyle.

Freedom to dream a great financial future.

Freedom to provide the best possible education for my child.

Freedom to maintain the same standard of living in the retirement phase.

Freedom to enjoy world tour after retirement.

Freedom to enjoy holidays every year from today.

Freedom to spend.

Freedom to invest.

Freedom from financial stress.

Freedom to follow the passion.

Freedom to pursue hobbies.

Freedom to give back to society.

Freedom to invest time with your dear ones.

Freedom to buy a diamond necklace.

Freedom to own a dream house.

Freedom to drive your dream car.

Freedom to fly in a private jet.

By far you know what is RRT, its causes and impacts on our overall financial life. And you also know how the overall financial health can impact your personal, family and social life.

Let's now understand the journey of overcoming the RRT and achieving financial freedom. What is freedom to you? Is it listed above? Or something else?

What do you think of its effect on physical and emotional well-being?

When we talk about Freedom, we don't mean to say that you don't need to work or you need to change your earning pattern or for that matter find some out of the box solution. Here we say that you need the steps given below to be able to earn that freedom and fulfill all your desires by working towards it with great will and persistence.

Once you are out of RRT then your journey will begin towards freedom. Freedom does not just mean to come out of RRT but it also means to always stay out of the race and keep moving in a direction towards your ultimate goal.

Retrospect yourself on the following situations:

- You are financially stressed.

- Don't know where you are heading.

- Looking for Short term happiness.

- Messed up with Income and Expenses.

- Fear of future.

- Always financially insecure.

- Every solution you bring comes with new problem.

So, what is the way out?

- Earn More?

- Change Company?

- Take Loan?

- Use Credit Card?

- Risky Investment?

- Additional Income?

- More hands and more hours of the day?

We have seen many horrifying traps until now. We are sure you must be thinking about a lot of different solutions for each trap. These different solutions for different traps may complicate your financial management. You may get confused about what to implement and how to implement it. One more chaos, now what to do? Do these types of different solution make my life simple?

Just imagine if you get a **Master Key** which will take you to freedom from all the traps. So many traps and one solution! Once you have this **Master Key** there is no need to think about any other solution. Just following this **Master Key** to Freedom for RRT will make your life simpler. If you are already in RRT, this **Master Key** will take you out of that RRT and help you to enjoy this freedom and pursue your goals. If you are a beginner then, **this Master Key will** protect you from RRT and give access to Freedom throughout.

Are you ready to welcome this Master Key in your life?

Let's start our journey to this **Master Key** which has 2 major milestones.

"THE JOURNEY TO A THOUSAND MILES BEGINS WITH THE FIRST STEP IN THE RIGHT DIRECTION!"

—RRT Freedom Expert (RRTFE)

CHAPTER
One

Milestone 1 – Realization

Till now you must have noted where all you have been trapped. We request you to go back, take a fresh recap which will help you to relate it with the solution. If you need a solution, then you need to Identify and acknowledge that there is a problem. **Assess your current financial health**. Having a problem statement is the basic ingredient to find out the solution. If you are ignorant or don't know that there is a problem then you will never be able to think or visualize that there could be a much better life than the one that you are having today. As a financial planner, we keep dealing with various individuals and families to guide them about the matters relating to personal finances. Sometimes we are really taken aback by the naivety or the ignorance of the people on the money matters.

The basic problem is that most of them are not aware that their financial life is already in a mess or is going to be in a mess in the future given their current lifestyle. We have seen people getting turned off when we show them the real financial mirror of their personal finances. Some of them will simply walk away. Few of them feel that if they follow the financial management system, they may not be able to enjoy today. They may have to do a lot of compromises. Some of them will argue that how this entire concept of financial planning itself is a big crap and is nothing more than an act of creating a fear monster.

Many of them keep the insurance agents, mutual fund (MF) distributors, stockbrokers and financial planners in the same bucket.

Oh! Ya and we forgot. Congratulations!! There are only a few people who complete the journey to this level. It clearly shows that you are really serious and ready to take responsibility for your financial life. You want to fulfill all your financial goals along with enjoying your present.

There are certain misconceptions about what it means to be financially free, some of them are:

I. **Financial Planning = Compromised Life.**

This is one of the big myths which keeps many people away from financial planning. But the reality is financial planning is a scientific structured process to enjoy your today and be prepared for enjoyable tomorrow.

II. **A big income will keep me out of debt and hence will make me financially free**.

What's the difference between someone who makes ₹ 50,000 a month and someone who makes ₹ 500,000 (5Lac) a month?

Answer: Nothing. Unless they have money set aside for emergencies and goals, they're both a pay check away from disaster.

Debt often rises with income. What keeps you out of debt isn't a high income but your spending and investing habits.

III. Rat Race Freedom is about drive fancy cars, wear fancy clothes, and live in fancy houses Trap Freedom is about

Not according to the folks who did a bunch of research and wrote books to be "The Millionaire". According to their studies, the people who have achieved rat race freedom drive an unexciting car, live in the same nondescript house they've owned for years and avoids designer labels. That's how they became millionaires and billionaires and achieved financial freedom.

So, who's buying all the designer clothes and Porsches? Many times, people will never become wealthy because they are swapping tomorrow's financial freedom for today's appearance. Life provides you the opportunity to either LOOK RICH or BE RICH. The choice is yours. The younger you decide the better. These people belong to Show Now, Save Later Category.

Shopping can really be fun, especially if you have money to spend or if you have those credit cards that are just simply waiting to be swiped. However, do you realize that every single purchase you make, you lose the money in an instant? Remember that it doesn't matter how little you save (& invest), as long as you do. Chances are, if you shop before you save, there might be nothing left to save since you might have spent it all.

We are not saying that a person seeking rat race freedom will never be able to drive fancy cars or own a big bungalow or can afford that glittering diamond necklace for his beloved wife. They surely can afford provided that they invest and grow money so big that this leisure and luxuries can be funded.

IV. **HAVING A JOB = FINANCIALLY SECURE**

This is actually what most people think and they are all wrong, because it is a fact, that a lot of people spend more than they earn. So even if you get a good amount of salary, at the end of the day, you'll realize, you have spent most of it, and you're struggling until the next pay check comes.

V. **BUDGET IS UNNECESSARY**

There are some people who think that having a certain budget is completely unnecessary since money is meant to be spent. It is actually a fact that money is indeed meant to be spent; however, it should be spent for the right reasons at the right time.

Without a budget, you could simply go crazy and buy everything you want, even if it should be the things that you need. Without a budget, there is a chance that you are not saving any. Without a budget, you are completely out of control, and at the end of the day, when you have spent it all, you'll eventually need it for some more significant reasons, and you wouldn't have any since you don't have a budget to follow.

COMMON MONEY BELIEFS

Freedom from RRT requires a complete paradigm shift now not only in terms of our spending and investing habits but it also needs a shift in our attitude towards money. What are our feelings about money? Do we treat money as a root of all evil? Do we think that having more money brings more worry than happiness? Unfortunately, our ancient literature also put money in a bad light by portraying it as the source of all evils. It is not uncommon to see in our society where spending on pampering the self or spouse or kids come with a feeling of guilt.

Let us draw your attention to certain **money myths** that are big mental blocks in achieving financial freedom.

I. **It Takes Money to Make Money**

Well, no doubt that having money can make it easier to make more money (if properly utilized) and is a bit more convenient as well. However, if you don't have money, it doesn't mean you can't make any. Plenty of big earners today and in history started off with very little money. You just need to put in some effort, some brains and be good at what you do. The key is to start with whatever you have and slowly make it big over a period of time.

On the contrary, there are plenty of examples where despite having ample wealth people have lost everything and came on the road because the money was not utilized properly.

II. **Money is the Root of Evil**

This old proverb is a pet peeve for us because it and the attitudes it engenders are the seeds of what make people averse to making money. Seeing money as some kind of enemy, or something that is difficult to work with, is like setting yourself up not to make any. Money is a tool like any other and these emotional connotations do not assist in the acquisition or use of that tool.

We think the proponents of this theory are mostly a group of people who are either too lazy to act to their potential and achieve superiority and better things in life or are too ignorant to understand the power behind money. We should ask them to look around and see what changes money can bring in the overall well-being of the society and country. So much of research is happening to find the cure for the life-threatening diseases, so much of work is happening to eradicate poverty, to provide education for children, to provide clean drinking water, food, and shelter to the people in remote villages, and so on. What is making this possible? The answer is **Money**. The likes of Bill Gates, Warren Buffett, and Tatas, to name a few, earned numerous wealth ethically throughout their life and now are using that money to bring the change in society.

These people are true philanthropists and the best of these give quietly and carefully, without much fanfare. Looking at their life and the simplicity, down to earth attitude do we still say that money is the root of evil? In fact, we will say that not having money is the real evil. Is the real cause behind many of the hardships and struggles.

III. **Time and Money are Proportionally Related**

This is again another common myth, a result of the industrial age and the model of employment it brought about. It works on the philosophy that you need to trade a good amount of time to earn the money. And the money earned will be proportional to the time that you are investing. Well, that is again not true.

If you are smart enough then you can multiply the money by hiring the people (the way businessman do) and trading their time. The Power of compounding also helps to grow your money exponentially if invested wisely.

IV. **If you're over a certain age, it's too late to achieve a financial freedom**

So of course, it's a lot easier to build up wealth throughout the course of your working years and by starting younger. Because it gives you time to invest more money and invested money itself gets more time to grow. But unfortunately, financial setbacks and other things in life sometimes get in the way. And if that's the case, it doesn't mean you're out of luck. It will require more discipline and other lifestyle adjustments but you can still achieve financial freedom. Once you begin to see it for what it is, your financial decisions can be based in reality and have a level of objectivity associated with them. Many people make stupid financial decisions because they have developed certain mindsets regarding money. Fears about losing money, or the idea that money is evil, simply don't help anyone.

Points to Ponder

Getting rid of these negative emotions, mental blocks and myths about the money is the key to achieve financial freedom. Always think right, do right and then see the real difference. Keep these proponents away from you who misled your thought process and prevent you from achieving your true potential.

It's never too late to plan for a better tomorrow. Start working towards your **Freedom from RRT** *today.*

CHAPTER
Two

Milestone 2 – Planning and Execution

Planning and Execution is one of the critical aspects to achieve rat race freedom once you have done an assessment of your current financial health.

We are very happy to introduce you to the **Master Key** to Freedom from RRT – Pyramid of Financial Success (PFS).

Pyramid of Financial Success is a scientific process of financial planning. For simplicity of understanding, this PFS is divided into 5 steps. Every step is interlinked with each other and support the upper step of PFS.

Pyramid of Financial Success:

Why Pyramid?

The Pyramid is considered as the strongest structure in the world. No natural calamity can easily break it. That's why the pyramids of Egypt are still going strong even after 5000 odd years.

Let's understand 5 steps of PFS:

1. FRM: To protect your Financial commitment from the unforeseen situations, events.

2. Enjoying today: Smart money management techniques to get maximum from today.

3. Proud Accomplishment: Taking care of all your family responsibilities which you had taken voluntarily.

4. Dream Life: Acquisitions and experiences adds flavours to your life.

5. Legacy: Helping your next generation to start a life at higher socio-economic level.

2.1. FRM (Financial Risk Management)

Most of us have built a house by using playing cards. What all did we check before starting to build it? Uniform and even Floor, the fan is off, windows are closed, looking for a wall nearby for the support, etc. Are you sure even after running these checks your playing card house was built strong and stayed for long? This all depends on how strong you built the first level of your house, that's the foundation. So, for any type of construction work first and most important part is a strong foundation. This strong foundation will ensure a long-lasting structure. This will protect the structure from all types of calamities. In the same way, a structure of Freedom to RRT has a strong foundation – Financial Risk Management (FRM).

An objective of FRM is to protect your financial liabilities and responsibilities from the unforeseen event. As a human being, you are exposed to many types of risks. Out of these risks, there are few which may result in a financial loss to you or to your family. FRM is a shield that protects the financial interests of you and your family in case of unseen and unpredicted circumstances.

Following are few situations where there is a possibility of financial loss.

- Death of breadwinner in family.
- Major Accidents causing death or disability.
- Illness, hospitalization
- Job Loss
- Natural Calamities
- Burglary
- Loss of property
- Third party liability
- Professional Liability

To protect financial loss from all such situations you need to have adequate FRM.

2.1.1. Financial loss due to death of bread winner

If family breadwinner dies there won't be any income to the family. This is a big loss for the family. Their survival, child education, existing loans all are at stake. Now it becomes important to protect the loss of future income of breadwinner and that can be done with the help of insurance.

Many people get confused with insurance as an investment which leads them to an RRT. Because return from this insurance as an investment fails to beat Enemy no. 1(We hope you know your Enemy no. 1. If you don't remember to refer Enemy no. 1 in the previous section). There is a good possibility of under insurance and low return if you consider insurance as an investment. Insurance should be taken only and only for protection. Hence when it comes to taking protection against financial loss due to death only **a Pure Term Plan** should be considered.

A pure Term plan is the most basic and must have insurance. In fact, only term insurance should be called as insurance in the right earnest. The insured amount is paid to the nominee in the event of the unfortunate death of an insurer.

So, check if you are covered with adequate term insurance. And if you are one of those 80% crowd who feel the term insurance is a waste of money and don't feel any need of it, then ask the below question to yourself:

If you go out on a solo vacation for 10 days, how much money would you leave behind for your wife, children and others who are financially dependent on you?

Say X amount for 10 days, maybe 1.5X amount for a month, and 3X for a year. What if you go on a solo trip forever(death)? How much do you think would they need? May be 10X so that they don't suffer from both financial and emotional loss at the same time?

What should that 10X amount be? There is a proper system of calculating this 10X amount which is also called a "Human Life Value" (HLV), this is calculated with respect to his or her earnings. Take the help of a Registered Investment Advisor, RRT Freedom Expert or Life Insurance Expert to get your HLV.

As a Thumb Rule, it is recommended that you should have 10 times of your yearly income as a life insurance cover. A pure Term plan is the cheapest Life Insurance available worldwide, you will get higher insurance cover for very less premium. Take cover equal to at least 10 times of yearly income i.e. "take-home salary" not your package, for people who are in business or profession, take at least 20 times your yearly income. (Because businessmen and professionals can show their expenses and have some other tax breaks.)

Always remember - 'Life insurance is not for you, but for those you love, who is going to live after you'. – RRT Freedom Expert

We had seen a lot of examples where once the breadwinner dies, the nightmare starts for the family, even in the joint family system. If one has not taken a proper cover for their financial liabilities, responsibilities then they gift a struggling life to their loved one. If you are a really responsible husband, responsible parent, responsible wife, responsible son or daughter and have a family that is financially dependent on you, then you need to have a proper life insurance cover for yourself.

2.1.2. Financial Loss due to Major Accidents causing death or disability

Life is very unpredictable and it can throw nasty surprises. Even walking on the road sometimes can prove to be fatal. It is no brainer that our country has a dubious distinction of leading the world in the number of road accidents. In some cases, this results in loss of life, and in other cases permanent or temporary disability ultimately paralyzing the normal life for an individual or household.

Every day you are traveling for business or work there is a possibility of accidents. If you met with an accident, you can come out safely or die or become permanently totally disabled (the Living Death, the most dangerous condition, where you will be living like a dead person) or partially disabled or temporarily totally disabled(paralysis, coma, major spinal cord injuries. Etc.). No one will continue you as an employee, you can't earn money, you won't be able to work, you won't be able to do the business in the same way. In these kind situations breadwinner of the family, the biggest asset of the family immediately turns into the biggest liability for the family.

It is a double whammy. Your income stops either temporarily or permanently, but your expenses increase multifold because of medicines, treatments, and rehabilitation.

A family will definitely look after you but they will need money for survival. As a generalized rule, this should be again as per the HLV or 10 times of your annual take-home income for salaried and 20 times for others.

2.1.3. Financial loss due to Illness, hospitalization

In case of illness, there is a possibility of expenses in the form of diagnostics, medicine, surgery, admitted to the hospital, etc. and such expenses need to be covered. Medical insurance can give this protection. Health insurance is also popularly termed as Mediclaim Insurance. This insurance is there to provide a financial cushion against such medical emergencies.

Medical inflation is inflation specific to the healthcare treatments and the medical insurance cover. The experience has been medical inflation generally runs at twice the country's inflation rate as a rough rule of thumb. What this means is medical treatment costs grow at double the normal inflation rate. As per the report by Mercer Marsh Benefits for the Year 2018, in India, the medical inflation was double the normal inflation rate and the trend will continue in the future as well.

With changing lifestyles, increased lifestyle diseases, an increase in life expectancy and advances in medical treatments the cost for health care keeps growing at the rate of 10% or more on a yearly basis. Also, bad health directly impacts your personal finance as it impacts your working and learning capability. Sometimes it may result in temporary job loss or pay loss as you may be required to take rest to recoup your health.

One should have health insurance equal to 50% of annual take-home salary and 100% of yearly earning for other than salaried.

There are many who are provided with medical insurance by companies. Do they also require to have a health cover? Yes, because this protection is to cover the most unfortunate event, there is a possibility that such a medical emergency may hit when you are in transit period where you do not have cover from any company.

You and your immediate family to be covered with medical insurance. RRT freedom expert suggests taking family floater cover if your age is less than 45 and individual cover to all if your age is more than 45.

You may wonder, why it is linked to earnings?

Well, with the advent of medical technologies and new sophisticated means of medical treatment, the cost of treatment is on the rise. Your lifestyle is also the function of your income. Ultimately this will govern your choice of healthcare center (hospital) in case of medical treatments.

So, cover yourself with adequate insurance so that you don't have to dip into savings that you may have allocated to some other financial goal.

2.1.4. Protection from Financial loss due to Job Loss

Emergencies don't come knocking on your door. That's why it is a must to have a protection corpus.

A protection fund is an accumulated pool of money that one can use towards any unforeseen contingencies that may arise. There are sudden large spends that can be catered to via adequate insurance like medical expenses, car damage, and theft. However, there are other emergencies like job loss which you cannot cater to other than from your savings. Unless you have systematically put aside an amount earmarked for such situations, you will have to dive into your long-term savings, which can collapse the pyramid of financial success.

It is advised to keep at least six months' worth of expenses aside as protection fund. This includes essential household expenses that are needed to run the family, utility bills, 50% of yearly insurance premiums, loan EMIs, 50% of annual children school & tuition fees, and discretionary expenses. You need to make sure all expenses are accounted for and add a little 5%-10% extra for miscellaneous expenses. Do make sure to review the amount required once a year, thanks to inflation. You may also need to review the corpus required whenever there is a substantial change in your income and expenses. This will ensure your protection fund will always be on track with your lifestyle.

Keep this amount in a secured type of instrument for protection, not growth, but the availability of the amount is important. Because it's a protection fund and protection can be required at any point in time. You can consider financial instruments like a Savings bank account, overnight fund, or short term Fixed Deposits. In case of a savings account - It will be advisable to move it to a separate joint savings bank account so that it is not accessible for daily use. This protection fund will not only protect you for the expenses but also protect you from making irrational decisions about your career.

Consult your RRT Freedom Expert to allocate your protection fund in these instruments.

A word of caution – Never consider credit cards as a protection instrument. You require protection funds in the most unfortunate time when you already are in trouble. Using a credit card in such a situation will attract one more trouble in your life. The interest charged on credit card dues, past payment date is ridiculously high and a person can easily fall under the debt trap. It can completely derail the personal finances of an individual or family.

2.1.5. Financial loss due to other risks

For burglary, property, financial loss of property due to natural calamities you are suggested to take property insurance, vehicle insurance (It is suggested to take comprehensive cover).

To cover the risk of third-party liability you have to have vehicle insurance, professional indemnity, director's liability cover. Once you are prepared with this FRM then you have a strong foundation to your Pyramid of Financial Success and you are protected from financial loss due to unforeseen events.

We suggest you analyze risks that you may come across, which might not have listed here and take proper protection for it.

Points to Ponder:

- Never invest in insurance for returns. Insurance is not an investment. It is a risk management tool.
- Thumb Rules
  - Take Term Cover equal to 10 times of your annual salary
  - Take Health cover equal to 6 times of your monthly salary
  - Take an accidental cover equal to 10 times of your annual salary
  - Maintain a protection fund equal to 6 times of your monthly expenses including loan EMI.

2.2. Today's Enjoyment

Once we visited one of our clients to plan their personal financial goals. They are a family of 3, the couple and a baby girl aged 4. We started discussing their money habits, spending habits. We were a bit shocked when we understood their spending habits. The couple looked to be a shopping addict leaving behind all basic financial senses. They were spending or purchasing anything they liked, without thinking whether they really need it or whether they will really use it. Just to give you an example – The baby had almost 20 odd pairs of footwear. A growing kid for whom the size of footwear will change fast and any pair will become useless within 6 to 9 months. They themselves agreed that some of the footwears are not used at all since the kid has grown in size. Those either needs to be thrown away or can be donated. What the couple is doing? Using their hard-earned money to make someone else rich.

So, this means, your impulsive, irrational, senseless buying is anRRT which will hold you from becoming financially free in life. Take a closer look at your closet or storeroom or better the loft. You will be surprised to notice how much garbage you have created in your home. How much cluttered your life is? There will be so many things you will find that you have barely used once or twice or may not have used it at all.

That Saree or lehenga or coat that you have shopped for your marriage, those showpieces that you would have collected during your honeymoon trip, those unused utensils, things that you might have purchased during sale, some "buy one get one free" scheme, stuff that you have bought thinking that you will need it someday in future. Alas! This is the story with most of our new clients whom we start to consult and I am sure you are no different. The impulsive buying, trying to find happiness in shopping. It's a big Trap.

2.2.1. "Rat Race Freedom - Needs and Wants Rule" (RRF-NW)

Liabilities come in the form of various Household expenses, Standard of living (Lifestyle) expenses, Loan servicing and completing financial commitments.

Don't worry we have a solution for the same. There is a simple formula that you can easily implement in your life if you want to take control of your Finances to get freedom from RRT. It just needs some tweaking to your shopaholic behavior.

Some of our clients who are actually following this rule are able to reduce their expenses by up to 30% without compromising their standard of living. Yes, you heard it right.

Read this carefully, and re-read if necessary. By following this rule, you can reduce your expenses by 30 % without changing your standard of living. we repeat "without changing your standard of living". Sounds

Interesting? We are not in favor of compromising the standard of living. At the same time ensuring that your money management strategies are right.

The rule is named as "Rat Race Freedom - Needs and Wants Rule" (RRF-NW). Now comes the question, "How do you identify what are your NEEDS and what are WANTS?"

This rule suggests that anything you think of buying or spending which is other than your basic necessities, regular requirements like weekly grocery, utility bills, etc. postpone it. Postpone it for **three times**. Even after 3 attempts of postponement if you feel to buy then go ahead because it is not your want it is your NEED now. But this rule comes with one condition that all of these attempts should not be done in one day. There should be a gap of at least a week between two attempts.

Why is that so? Because it will take you a month to buy that product, and meanwhile maybe you realize that you can easily manage things without that product.

A simple but effective formula. Try to execute it and see the results. Reduce your expenses to 70% or 80% without compromising on the standard of living.

Start with small things. Like one of our clients did. She was fond of online shopping. Every week or month she would do some shopping online and would hardly use those products. So next time when she came across a big shopping sale at one of the e-commerce sites and selected a few cosmetics, clothes and sandals. But before checking out she applied this rule of RRF-NW and to her amazing she actually did not need any of those things. As a result, she emptied her cart and closed the app. To her surprise, she did not even feel like buying it the next month when it was half of the original price, because she already had many. So, without compromising on her standard of living she could bring down her lifestyle expenses by postponing the urge to shop. Rule RRF-NW will ensure that you give up your habit of buying redundant or unwanted stuff. A great way to reduce the unused things at your home and declutter your life.

Give it a shot. It's worth.

One more thing we recommend is to start monitoring your expenses, write it down. You will soon be able to identify as to what is it that is creating a big hole in your coffer. This will start giving you control over your expenses and help you to spend wisely, save wisely and invest wisely.

In many of our Financial Planning Awareness camps, one common question asked by participants is how to allocate my earnings? Considering this, after knowing how to reduce your expense without compromising your standard of living, now we would like to give you one more important pointer of Financial Planning ratios. "What should be the proportion of expenses, loans, and savings to your income?"

We suggest you can spend up to 30% of your take-home salary (or your monthly income) for your Expenses. This will include regular household expenses + standard of living expenses + child education expenses + dependent expenses if any.

Expense to Income Ratio < 30%.

This % may vary by +/- 5% industry to industry, income growth.

A few more good habits to inculcate, read your salary slip, bank statements, and credit card statements and understand where your money is going. Are there any additional charges applied to you? Choose a bank with minimum savings account charges for additional services. You can find these charges on the bank's website. Check if you can move to another financial institution where these charges are minimum for the transactions which you do frequently. Before you issue someone a cheque, make sure that its account payee and you have enough balance in your account to avoid check the bounce penalty. Maintain the required average monthly balance.

2.2.2. Invest in Self and Grow your income.

Coming to the next important question "if my expenses are more than the given limits, then how to manage it?"

Even after doing all this, if you are not really able to control your expenses then the only alternative is to increase the value of the best asset that you have. Now, which is the best asset that you have? You may answer it as your house, equity investments or gold. No no no... we are not talking about that. This is an asset that every individual owns and it's God gifted plus it increases your income.

The best asset that anyone has is "Self".

Yes. It's you, yourself. The best asset that you have is you, yourself. You agree to this, right? If you just revise your life and see what value add you have done to yourself then you will understand. e.g. when you were a kid you learned crawling, walking and jumping by doing those things again and again. It made you ready for the next step of going to school. Then you went to school and learned that made you ready for college and now all this learning over a period of 15-16 years made you capable to help you earn. But what happened after getting a job? Did you still continue to learn new skills to be ready to take up the next responsibilities? If your answer is No, then by this small recap, you would have realized that for growing up you need continuous learning.

And this is why we say that the best asset is yourself. To get good returns from this asset increase its value. How value can be increased? Simply by putting effort to gain knowledge.

Learning different skills like soft skills, technical skills or any other skills related to your field having good demand in the market can increase your value. Take all those efforts which you can to sharpen your skills and knowledge. Upgrade yourself to the next level of employability or Business expansion or professional excellence.

Invest in SELF and Grow your income.

* S – Be **SKILLFUL**
* E –Be **Emotionally** Fit
* L – Be **LUCID**
* F – Be at **FOREFRONT** of Self development

2.2.3. Investment to Income

There is a difference in savings and investments. Savings is just keeping money idle lying in savings account whereas investments is where it starts growing more than inflation.

Income – Expenses on needs = Investments

How to identify Needs? You already know it from RRF-NW rule.

Investment to Income more than 25%.

Also remember, whenever there is an increase in salary increase your investments as well.

Once you know how much amount is available to invest, where and how to invest we will see in the coming chapters.

2.2.4. Wisely choose your loans

The loans can be categorized as bad loans and good loans. Bad loans are the ones that take out money from your pocket and at the end of this loan, you are in loss. These are the loans where the rate of interest is high and tenure is less. These types of loans are used to spend on lifestyle expenses or luxuries or to purchase some depreciating assets. Credit Card loans, Vehicle loans, personal loans fall in this category.

Are there good loans also? Yes. There are. These loans are designed to make you RICH. These loans come with a lower rate of Interest and a long duration. The good loans are invested to build an appreciating asset. Examples of these loans are a home loan, education loan. On top of that, there are tax benefits offered by the government which further reduces the effective interest rate.

An Education Loan is an investment in yourself or your child's future. Also, interest paid on this loan is considered for the tax benefit which is an additional bonus.

So how much should be the limit for taking loans? As a rule of thumb, EMI for your all loans put together can be up to 45% of your take-home income. To customize your own EMI limit, consult a Rat Race Trap Freedom Expert.

EMI to Income Ratio < 45%

If there is no EMI then what will you do with this money? Most of you may think that we can use this amount to spend. No!! This should go into investments. Because if you are young and have not taken any loan that means that you are preparing yourself for the loans may be a housing loan. To accumulate this amount to pay the margin money and if you are near to retirement then use this fund to increase your retirement kitty so that you can enjoy your retirement.

Points to Ponder

Financial Planning Ratios	
Expense to Income	< 30%
Loans to Income	< 45%
Savings to Income	> 25%

- Inculcate the habit of writing your expenses. Remember to keep it simple. Define broad level categories and segregate your expenses under these categories. E.g. Household Expenses, Lifestyle expenses, Dependents Expenses, Insurance premiums.

- Allocate some amount of your income for your personal growth, enhancement of professional skills. That will increase your market value and will help you to earn more by keeping you one step ahead of your peers or competitors.

2.2.5. Liabilities

2.2.5.1. Pay down bad loans

Follow the steps below to clear your bad loans.

1. Make a list of all your bad loans.

2. Arrange those loans in order from higher rate of interest to the lowest.

3. Continue your regular EMIs of all loans.

4. Any additional balance after completing your investment target put it to clear the loan on top of your list.

5. Once that first loan is paid off, again start from step no. 1.

6. Run through these steps 1-5 till all your loans are paid off.

There are some yardsticks which you can follow.

- Price of home can be up to 5 times of your yearly family take home income.

- Price of car can be up to 50% of your yearly family take home income.

- Price of your mobile can be up to 25% of your monthly take home income.

- Price of two-wheeler can be up to 100% of your monthly take home income.

- Expenses of your all vacations in a year can be up to 100% your monthly take home income.

*Take Home Income: It's your income after tax. It's an amount that gets deposited in your bank account and is available to spend.

2.2.5.2. How not to get into Credit Card Trap

Given below certain points for your benefit-

- Do not get a credit card. Even if you want to have, never own more than one credit card. Close those extra cards properly by paying off the balance amount and with written confirmation.

- Make sure the limit on your credit card is half of your monthly take-home income.

- Never use a credit card to withdraw cash. The rate of interest starts immediately the day you withdraw cash along with other charges if any.

- Try to use your Debit card for offline purchases and net banking for online purchases. This will make sure that you can purchase only to the limit of your bank balance. It helps to gain control over the cash flow position & control your spending habits.

- Keep credit cards at home when you plan to go for window shopping. Every human being craves for instant gratification and making some unplanned or big purchase to pamper yourself or your near and dear ones, for which you don't have to pay immediately, is very tempting and difficult to resist.

- Take a credit card from a bank where your main account is. Initiate a standing instruction to your bank account to settle 100% of your due amount and not a minimum payment of credit card bill on the due date

- Make it a habit to check monthly credit card statement & raise any inaccuracies with the credit card company immediately.

- Check your CIBIL score annually to make sure that any credit cards which are closed/ not in your name are still not open.

- In case of loss of credit card, report it immediately to the company and get it closed. Ask for the Service Request number for your future reference.

- If you have a higher credit limit for your credit card take insurance for it.

- Never hand over your credit card to anyone including your spouse, girl/boyfriend or friend. You may end up receiving a huge unexpected bill. It is not legal as well. Beware: they say – A friend in need is a friend indeed does not work here. Better safe than sorry.

2.2.5.3. When can I buy a home?

If you want to get freedom from the rat race trap then create the asset first, don't go for loans. Buying a home at the beginning of one's career is the liability that young couples are creating for themselves.

First, think about whether you are going to stay where your job or business is for the rest of your life. If No then never think of buying a home.

Buying a home is more of an emotional decision than the practical one. People tend to succumb to the pressure from parents, in-laws, relatives, friends, etc. Many people take home as a prestige point.

So, if it is a must to buy a home, then you should first fix your budget. For your first home, the budget should not be more than 5 times your annual income. There is no need to buy a bigger home. You can buy a small home first and then once you have created a good asset base then you can move on to a bigger one. There are some stupid notions in our country – something like we buy a home only once in a lifetime so it should be the best fit for all our needs and luxuries. But now this is passed. This is where people shop for a bigger house, bite more than they can chew, and then end up paying heavy monthly EMI, ending up with a lot of financial, and emotional stress. Great interior and furniture create an additional hole in the pocket and people start leading a compromised life.

Normally home is there to provide peace of mind and relaxation. But what's happening here? Exactly reverse. The bigger home and costly interior come with a lot of worries, stress and financial inconvenience.

So, for the people who want to follow proper financial discipline, want to create an asset first, how they should prepare themselves so that they can buy a home?

The first thing you should accumulate at least twice your yearly income as reserves for home. 70% of that would be utilized for Margin money (down payment) for home and remaining for registration, furniture, and other expenses.

For example, if you are earning ₹ 10 lakhs a year, then the home which you can buy can be up to ₹50 lacs and you should have ₹20 lacs in your pocket. So around ₹10 lacs will go as a down payment,₹10 lacs for registration and basic furniture.

Normally investor goes to buy ₹50 lacs home with having ₹5 lacs in the pocket, and then they keep on taking loans, soft loans from their parents/relative/friends, or personal loan for interiors and other expenses. With this EMI goes almost 80% to 90% leaving a very little behind for their financial comfort. Such people buy a palace and live like a beggar as they don't have anything to provide for. If this is your scenario you made your builder RICH at the cost of your happiness.

Points to ponder:

- Find out which is your bad loan and pay it off first.

- Do not use credit cards.

- Find out if buying a home is your emotional decision or a need.

- Cost of the home should not be more than 5 times of your annual income.

- If you decide to buy a home prepare yourself first.

2.3. Proud Accomplishment

The first and foremost in this category is your responsibility towards you. Yes, you heard it right. Taking care of yourself tops the list. So, what does it mean in the context of personal finance? It means creating funds for your future so that when you stop working you can still enjoy the luxuries of life and maintain your standard of living. We are talking about the retirement fund. So, creating funds for your retirement takes the highest priority. What this means is that in case if funds are not available even for a very important goal like funding your child education then retirement funding takes priority. After which comes to child education and then your other goals, aspirations.

2.3.1. Retirement Fund

A time in your life would come, where you will stop working so your income will be **zero** but expenses will continue and will grow with each passing year. This is where your planning for future comes.

They say, 'half knowledge is no knowledge'. In the same way 'half-job done is no job done"

Now let's see what happens if you don't plan or just do halfway plan for your retirement.

1. You have to work for your whole life. Working the iwhole life is good when you do that with passion and not because you need to meet your basic needs. If you don't plan well and don't consider all

the factors right, you would land up working till you die.

2. You may outlive your expectation of survival age, if you are not prepared with the right amount of retirement fund then you have to end your sunset years in poverty. There are so many examples like Parvin Babi, Meena Kumari, AK Hangal, Bismillah Khan of people who were extremely rich and popular at a time, but died in poverty.

3. You won't be able to enjoy retired life. If you want to enjoy a relaxed life, go on vacation, continue to stay in your dream house, then plan your retirement first.

4. Many of the times people take an emotional decision and decide to pass their residential house to the next generation. But it's not required because you never know where your children are going to stay, whether they will be staying with you. Maintaining this property may be time-consuming and tedious for them. The house in which you stay cannot be considered as an asset but it can be allocated to your goal of retirement with the help of Reverse Mortgage.

So now that we know the why's and what's, let's see how to plan it. We might get some basic questions like:

- How much is enough for retirement?
- How do I know I have sufficient funds for retirement?

- What sort of retirement plan should I have that will help me save for retirement?

- What can retirement/financial planners do to help me with my retirement?

- How much money is it safe to draw down from my retirement fund?

- How do I know how long my retirement funds will last?

There are lot more questions and doubts if you start thinking in more detail. These questions can be solved by calculating the amount required for retirement.

Retirement fund requirement calculations:

Factors to be considered for calculation of retirement fund.

1. Today's expenses for consideration of retirement.

2. Rate of inflation till retirement and post retirement

3. Rate of return till retirement and post retirement

4. No. of years till retirement and post retirement

1. Today's expenses for consideration of retirement:

Today's expenses include household, lifestyle, Life Insurance, loan EMI, Kids' expenses like for kids schooling, classes and hobbies, dependent parents/siblings. But at the time of retirement your expenses such as loan EMI,

Life insurance premium would not be there. Your kids and parents may not be your dependent as well. Following table will give you a foresight on how your expenses would be reduced based on the size of your family. You can deduct this amount from your total current expenses.

No. of dependents	*Reduction factor in %*
0	0%
Up to 2	25%
2-4	35%
More than 4	45%

There are some expenses which are fixed and some are variable expenses. Variable expenses can be reduced depending on no. of dependents. Fixed expenses such as property tax, electricity bill. Etc. Won't have any effect as those are fixed. You can use the following formula to calculate Today's expense.

Today's Expenses for the consideration of Retirement =

(Today's total expenses – Loan EMI – Life insurance premium – Dependent Expenses) * reduction factor in %

Even after deduction of dependent expenses, few expenses (medical expenses, school expenses …etc.) which are inbuilt in household and standard of living expenses. Hence this reduction factor is used to calculate..

There are two phases to retirement planning namely Accumulation phase and Distribution phase:

Responsibility of your own retirement starts from your birth. Accumulation phase usually starts from the day you start earning. During the accumulation phase you are earning and you start accumulating for your retirement. The day you retire your income becomes zero. But your expenses continue and it also grows as per your standard of living and inflation.

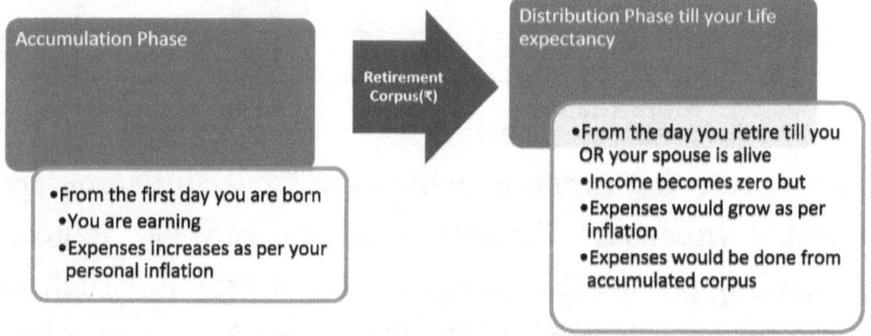

1. Accumulation: It's a stage at which the saving and investment for the retirement corpus are made.

   It has 3 important factors:

   a. **Timing**: - The earlier you start, the better. Your investments get that much time to grow for you and become a strong pillar and support at the right time.

      The below graph explains how if someone starts to invest₹25000 monthly from age of 25 or 35 or 40 then how much would be accumulated when he reaches his retirement age of 60. Assuming he gets a return of 12% see how much wealth is created. And if someone who delays his investment by 10-15 years how much he could lose. It doesn't mean that you cannot start your investment after the age 25 but it is to showcase you how much you lose just by a delay of 5-10 years.

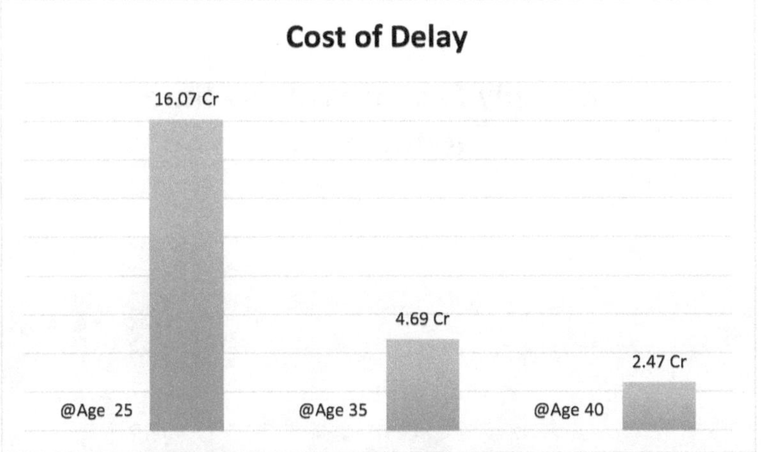

b. **Inflation:** Which inflation will you consider to determine how much you need for retirement? Do you remember your Enemy no. 1? Yes. It's a Personal Inflation from Part 2.

See the graph below to find the difference in requirement of monthly expenses at the time of retirement. Considering **the right Inflation rate is the key** while arriving at your retirement fund. If you fail to consider this correctly then you may end up in creating insufficient retirement fund which leads to old age poverty.

Graph Below graph shows huge difference between Monthly Expenses increasing at Basic Inflation Rate = 6% and monthly expenses increasing at Personal Inflation Rate = 11%.

Considering ₹ 30,000 of today's expenses and 35 years to retire

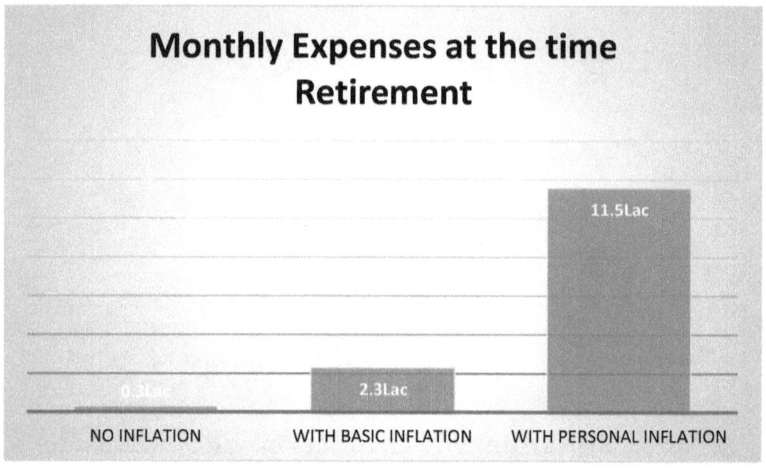

The below graph shows the difference when you invest without considering inflation what your corpus might be, and when you consider basic inflation of 6% and personal inflation of 11% how much your corpus should be.

Graph: Corpus Requirement at the start of retirement considering 30 Years during distribution phase.

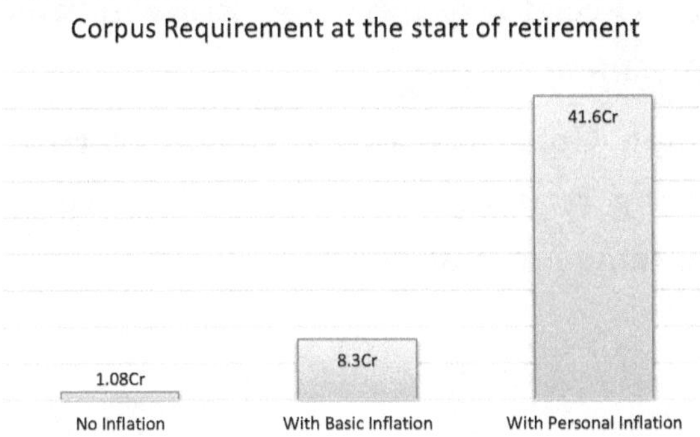

So, if Inflation is considered as 0 or 6% then you may end up in poverty during the time of retirement.

c. **Expenses**: You need to consider all kinds of expenses like household, lifestyle. Many people think that they would be living a simple lifestyle after retirement. They won't be going for extravagant shopping and luxury travelling. But that is no truer as trend is changing and people like to maintain at least the same kind of lifestyle.

Graph: Underestimating expenses, Cut short expenses of ₹30000 by 33% to ₹20000.

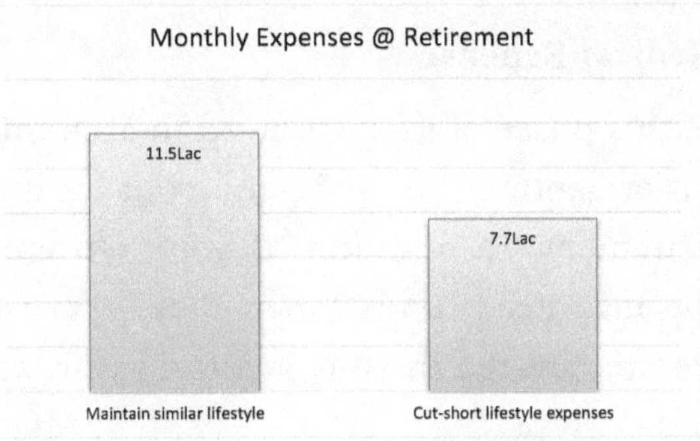

Now check the graph below to see its effect on the retirement corpus.

Graph: Corpus requirement considering 30 years during retirement. Inflation and RoR remains the same for simplicity.

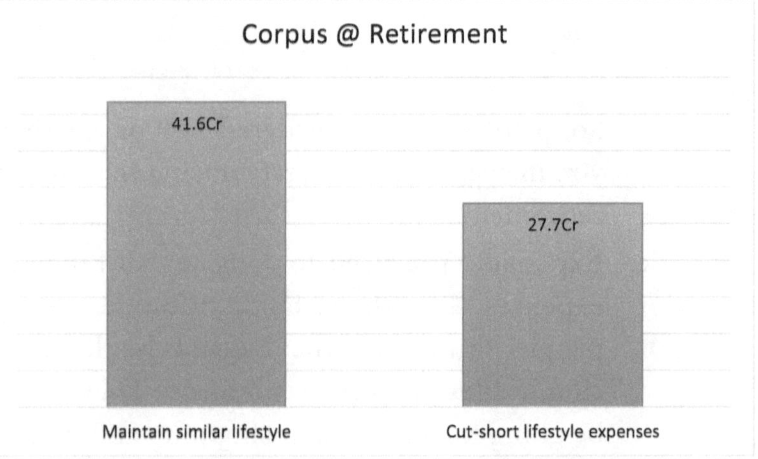

If any of these 3 factors is considered incorrectly then your corpus amount would vary and may not be sufficient for you. So be very careful when you plan for this. Better take a Rat Race Freedom Experts help.

Medical Expenses:

At this phase of life, you need to accumulate for a buffer amount to maintain your health during retirement. In addition to your retirement fund you may need funds for medical expenses which are not covered in your medical insurance. Funds required would be 20% of the retirement funds you have planned.

2. Distribution phase:

This is a phase where you should start living your life for yourself. Till this time, you were working for fulfilling your liabilities and responsibilities. Till date everything is done and now you have a time for yourself for enjoyment of your life. At this point if you have a right kind of financial backup you can really turn this time into a memorable time of your life. You can enjoy all that things which you could not do till today because of your liabilities, responsibilities and time challenge. You can choose to contribute time to the society, pursue your hobbies, enjoy tours, spend time with your loved once or whatever you were dreaming about.

Now you have a choice at this junction of life and this option depends on how much funds are available with you for your retirement. The options are

1. You can compromise on your standard of living

2. You can maintain the same standard of living

3. Upgrade the standard of living.

One point you have to keep in mind is that even if you are retired your Enemy No. 1 is not. So even if you choose to maintain your standard of living you will need more and more amount every year. So, retirement fund should be sufficient to take care of growing expenses even after retirement. One could think about this phase is, the inflation rate is having only 2 effects, one is price rise and second is standard of living. If you choose to maintain your standard of living then you have only one effect.

The distribution stage of retirement is when the corpus created in the accumulation stage is employed to generate the income required to meet expenses during retirement. The investment made at this stage is primarily income-oriented.

a. **The Period for which corpus would last:** It is up to you how you will be consuming your corpus. But your consumption rate of corpus would decide how long your corpus would last and whether it would be sufficient till you survive.

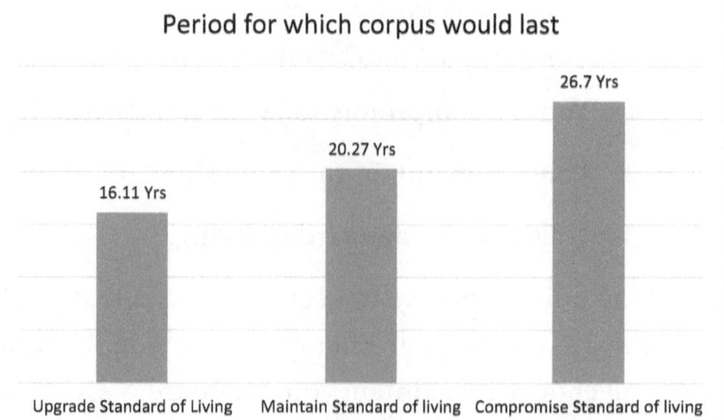

b. Post-tax rate of interest (RoI during distribution phase): Check where and how much to invest, and tax benefits available. Wisely choose the best for yourself. E.g. Compare FD with Debt mutual funds. If you need amount before maturity then you need to break your FD, whereas you can withdraw it from most of the debt MFs.In FD Tax is applicable even on accrued interest which hasn't been received hence finally the income that compounds in case of MFs is greater. This may seem easy to read but difficult to execute and choose the right way of investment. For the same we recommend you to take the help of financial planner or RRTFE.

In the earlier part of this book, we have seen that the house that you are staying in is not your Asset but a liability, as to maintain a property you need to spend money. Consider now you are above 60 years of age and the amount accumulated is not sufficient for the rest of the years in the distribution phase. Then you have one solution, and that is your house where you are living. You can reverse mortgage this property and it can help you earn the amount on a monthly basis or lump sum and you can still live in that house till you are alive. You can do it by taking a loan against it with a bank or housing finance company. After you and your spouse's death if your kids want to they can take possession of this house by paying the pending dues.

2.3.2. Responsibility: Child education and marriage

When it comes to the grooming of kids, education tops the list in the minds of every parent. Parents dream to give the best education to their child starting right from the nursery. The rising cost of education is an aspect that every parent needs to keep in mind and they should plan their finances accordingly.

It is common to have annual expenses of ₹50 thousand to ₹1 lac for a nursery or pre-school including tuition fees, bus, books, uniforms, etc. The professional courses after 12th like engineering, medical, management can cost anything from ₹10-25 lacs and above. On top of that, there are expenses for post-graduation which also requires almost the same amount for 2 years. And if its abroad it may require 2 to 5 times of graduation expenses.

When it comes to preparation for child education expenses, many people think it's far away so why to bother now? In reality, the object appears far is not actually that far.

If you use the time wisely and invest for education from the date of birth itself, 3 great things happen to your investment:

i. Power of compounding: Investments get time to grow. As your child grows, the same way your investment grows and helps you complete your kid's education goals.

ii. As you have a long time, you have to make a small amount of investment so it's not heavy on your pocket now or later.

iii. More the tenure of the investment allows to take more risks to get higher returns.

Following table shows how much you need to invest if at right time or with delay, where you need ₹1cr to fund your child's post-graduation expenses.

Post-Graduation Investment			
Investment started at child's age	0	5	10	15
No. of years to accumulate corpus	22	17	12	7
Amount to accumulate grows as per inflation	₹ 1,00,00,000		
RoR	15%	14%	12%	10%
Investment required per month	₹ 4,890	₹ 12,081	₹ 31,342	₹ 82,679
Choice of asset class	100% Equity	80% Equity 20% Debt	50% Equity 50% Debt	100% Debt

From the chart above, it's very clear, how smart move it will prove to be if you plan for child's education right from their birth or even better from the day you come to know you are going to be parents. In the same way, you can plan for their marriage too.

No need for loan: Right amount is available at the right time, so no need to go for educational loan. Check the following table if you want ₹ 1 cr for your son after his post-graduation after 22 years, you can easily do it if you invest ₹ 5000 for 22 years.

Impact on Loan				
Invested for (Yrs.)	22	17	12	7
Invested monthly (Approx.)	5000	5000	5000	5000
Accumulated amount (Approx.)	₹1 Cr	₹ 41 lac	₹ 16 lac	₹ 6 lac
Loan Amount (Approx.)	0	₹ 58 lac	₹ 83 lac	₹ 93 lac
EMI Loan (Approx.)	0	₹ 0.76 lac	₹ 1.1 lac	₹ 1.24 lac

2.3.3. Taxes are Good

Yes! It sounds weird but it means that you are earning and you are paying the government to give you facilities and keep you earning money. As a government-created, an environment for making businesses start to grow and expand. That's why you are getting an opportunity to earn money. If you are in business or self-employed there is a possibility that you create employment which is actually a job of government. As you are doing their work government gives more tax breaks. But if you are an employee you take advantage of the government's created infrastructure and that's why you have very limited tax breaks. Now whenever you think of tax, think beyond taxation. Think of wealth creation. If you are focused on tax-saving after the specific limit of exemptions you may get frustrated because you can't save tax. This negativity may affect your income generating capability. So be happy in earning more and pay taxes.

Remember only 2 things are certain in this world, and those are Death and Tax. So, don't avoid paying taxes. Always pray to be the highest Tax Payer, as that means you are the highest earner as well. Also always remember don't buy things in a hurry to save tax and consider tax as a friend who gives you a push to earn more. Refer to your CA for tax planning.

2.3.4. Put your horse before the cart

Now we are sure that you know where and how to use your money. First 30% for your expenses, and next 40% for Loan servicing (if any). If you don't have Loan then 40% of your loan amount should go in Investments and not in expenses. Do not use this amount for increasing lifestyle expenses. Using this surplus amount to increase the standard of living will take you in the Income – Expenses trap.

We have seen many cases where both life partners are working, the expenses are according to their total income. On some fine day one partner quits the job to focus more on family commitments, the income drops almost 50%. But expenses continue. It is very easy to increase the standard of living with the surplus money but when income drops for whatsoever reason it is difficult to go back original lifestyle. Your body by now would be accustomed to luxuries, comfort and it's not that easy to give away those comforts so easily. This also could burn a major hole in the retirement kitty during the accumulation phase. As a standard rule, you need to have 30% of investible surplus after taking care of your routine expenses, responsibilities, and loans. The more it is the better.

Where to invest in, the next question that many people have. Is that the right question?

Investment instruments (Products) are merely the vehicle. It is not the destination in itself. The destination is the financial goal that you want to achieve with that investment. So, the basic question should be for **what to invest and what is the duration for that goal?** E.g. if your goal is to invest in your child's education (graduation) and your child is 2 years old then your goal duration could be 15 years. If your goal is international vacation then your goal duration could be one or two or maybe 3 years.

Having clarity on these aspects will help you to decide where to invest and select the best investment avenue that could maximize your returns if the goal is long term and protect your capital by providing modest returns if your goal is short term.

If you follow this to set each goal you shall clearly come to know how much time you have to reach the goal, the corpus you would need, and where and how you can invest for it and accordingly select the asset class or investment tool.

Till now we discussed the basic responsibilities and liabilities and the financial risk management structure. Following are the parameters which you can use to decide Investment Tool and make your base strong

1. Goal

2. Time for the goal

3. Corpus needed for the goal

All 3 put together shall help us decide the strategy to use different investment tools.

Warning: If you don't stick to your goal and investment the base/structure shall go weak and shall pull you down. Changing strategy is a good thing to do, but changing the goal in between because the old strategy is not working is not at all the right thing to do

2.3.5. Asset Class

As we have seen in chapter 8 of Part 2 of this book there are, five different asset classes i.e. Cash, Debt, Gold, Real Estate, Equity. Let's map these Asset classes(where most of investment tools fit in) to the goals based on the tenure of the goal.

Based on the tenure of the goal you can classify the goals into 4 different categories.

1. Ultra-short term (Within 3 months or for which you cannot specify the duration)

2. Short Term (3 months to 3 Years)

3. Mid Term (3 Years to 10 Years)

4. Long term (More than 10 Years)

Now once you classify your goals in categories you can choose right asset class to invest to achieve the goal, you have to review this allocation at least once in a year because the duration of the goal will change hence the goal category.

Many people suggest to have diversified investment management, but if you have goal-based investment then there is no need to go for diversification. In fact, with goal-based investment, the portfolio will emerge as a diversified portfolio automatically.

Goals Tenure	Category of Goal	Asset Class
0 to 3 Months	Ultra-short term	Cash
3 months to 3 Yrs.	Short Term	Debt
3 Yrs. to 10 Yrs.	Mid Term*	Debt + Equity
10 Yrs. +	Long Term	Equity

*Mid Term goal: During this phase you have to keep on reducing equity exposure when duration goes down. The whole strategy is to bring down equity exposure from 100% to 0% and increase the debt exposure from 0% to 100%. So, when this mid-term goal changes to short term goal your all invested amount is in 100% debt.

For long term goal as the duration is high you can take exposure towards higher risk equity investments like mid cap and small cap.

Disclaimer*: This allocation may vary from person to person in consideration of income generating capacity and wealth created till date. To set your customized allocation meeting RRFT expert or a Financial Planner is recommended.*

Many investors assume that there is a BIG risk in investing with equity. But equity is an asset class which has a potential to deliver good returns as compared to any of these 5-asset class. Then there is a dilemma whether to invest in equity or not. But with the strategy given above you can get advantage of equity when it comes to returns and advantage of debt when it comes to completion of goal. This simple strategy of allocation depending on category of goal can take you towards achievement of your goals.

This way we can manage the risk well and achieve your goals and be proud of your accomplishments. By now we know how to plan for the goal, now we know which kind of asset mix we need for every kind of goal. Check Annexure for quick planner page where you can plan your goals.

2.3.6. Calculate Rate of return

Mainly there are 3 types of returns.

2.3.6.1. Absolute Return

This return shows what percentage the asset has achieved over a certain period of time. This measure looks at the appreciation or depreciation. It is the amount that an asset gains/loses over a period of time. It is expressed in percentage. The formula to calculate absolute returns:

$$\text{Absolute return} = \frac{(\text{Current value} - \text{Purchase value})}{\text{Purchase value}} \times 100$$

For example, if you had invested ₹4500 in a fund and redeemed when the value was ₹5100, you would have made a gain of ₹600, which is 13.33% of the amount invested. This is the absolute return you got from the investment.

2.3.6.2. Compounded Returns (CAGR)

This is a return on return. Here profits are reinvested at the end of each year. Here returns may not be the same each year. It shows how the investment would have grown had it generated a steady return.

Let's now see how CAGR can be quickly computed using an excel file. Here, we consider CAGR of investment made in MF. Assuming you had invested ₹ 1 lakh in an MF three years back at a NAV of ₹ 20. Now, the NAV is ₹ 40.

Here's the formula

= (((ending-value/beginning-value) ^(1/number-of-years)) – 1*100

So, it will be

= (((40/20) ^ (1/3))-1) *100

And on hitting enter, the result is:

= 25.99% Or you use RATE function in excel.

CAGR is the most common returns used for comparison of assets.

2.3.6.3. IRR (Internal Rate of Return):

Cash inflows and outflows may not always be evenly matched and instead these could be at irregular intervals. For example, in a money-back plan or in a mutual fund SIP. For that we can use the XIRR function. Use XIRR Function in Excel for calculating internal rate of return or annualized yield for a schedule of cash flows occurring at irregular intervals.

2.3.7. Apple to Apple Comparison

Now you know the concept of Time Value of Money and you have seen how the value of money varies with time. Let's see how to use it for comparing financial products.

Whenever there is a Financial Product at your doorstep or you are searching for a financial product compare them. There should be an apple to apple comparison. What's this apple to apple comparison for any financial product? Consider following parameters for comparison. First is Tenure for which amount would be invested and second is RoR

Apple to apple comparison means, comparing one investment with other investment when both are having same tenure and same investment amount. Then only this comparison will take you to the right investment decision.

Take an example of 3 long term investments i.e. PPF, Insurance and MFs

1. Let's compare these 3 products to invest for 16 years (Note here you have to consider same tenure for all 3 products.) Returns expected are PPF 8.1%, Insurance Policies 4-5% and Equity 10 to 15% per annum. (Note here returns are calculated in the same way. I.e. CAGR.)

2. Consider you invest in all three instruments. After 5 years PPF and insurance policies will give you expected returns, but MFs returns may vary in short term it could be negative or less than 5% or more. You cannot compare these instruments before completing the tenure as these are different kinds of products. You cannot compare the returns as MFs are linked with market and is a long-term investment instrument. But yes, you can compare internal funds to check which MFs is doing better. Comparing MF to MF or One insurance plan to other insurance plan is right, if you compare MF to

PPF in between tenure then you will not get a clear picture as they work with different parameters.

3. Now if you compare the returns in PPF with equity investments make sure that both are calculated in same manner. There are 3 ways in which the returns can be calculated, CAGR or absolute or IRR (Internal Rate of Return) as seen in the previous topic. While comparing products make sure that their returns are calculated in the same way. And then only compare it.

2.3.8. Power of Compounding

Use Excel to make the calculation of say you investing ₹ 5000 every month and earning 14% Rate of return and check the answer. Now do the same for various tenures. With additional increase of 5 years can multiply your income multifold.

Invested Amount	RoR	Tenure (Yrs.)	Total Invested Amount	Maturity Amount	No. of times investment increased by
₹ 5,000	14%	5	₹ 3,00,000	₹ 4,36,004	1.45
₹ 5,000	14%	10	₹ 6,00,000	₹ 13,10,457	2.18
₹ 5,000	14%	15	₹ 9,00,000	₹ 30,64,269	3.40
₹ 5,000	14%	20	₹ 12,00,000	₹ 65,81,731	5.48
₹ 5,000	14%	25	₹ 15,00,000	₹ 1,36,36,389	9.09
₹ 5,000	14%	30	₹ 18,00,000	₹ 2,77,85,278	15.44

There must be something amazingly true about its power so only the great Albert Einstein called "compounding interest as the eighth wonder of the world"

But there are 2 rules, if you follow them then only this shall work in your favor

1. **Don't panic:** when the market goes volatile, just wait and let the compounding show its magic

2. **Give Time:** Miracles don't happen suddenly, slowly they start happening and after a long term suddenly become big…just like the Chinese bamboo. In its first year though, we see no visible signs of growth in spite of providing required nutritional things. In the second year (again), there is no growth above the soil.

The third, fourth year…still, shows no sign of anything happening.

Our patience is tested, and we begin to wonder if our efforts caring for and watering the tree will ever be rewarded. We start to doubt ourselves and question the value of our efforts. Inevitably, we contemplate quitting. But then finally in the fifth year – something amazing happens…

The Chinese Bamboo Tree grows 80 feet tall in just six weeks!

But think for a moment, does the Chinese Bamboo Tree really grow 80 feet in six weeks? Did the Chinese Bamboo Tree lie dormant for four years only to grow exponentially in the fifth? Or, was the little tree growing underground, developing a root system strong enough to support its potential for outward growth in the fifth year and beyond?

In the same way your investments need time to grow, you won't get immediate returns, you might feel it's not worth holding it, but if the Chinese bamboo farmer would have felt the same and would have dug up his little seed every year to see if it was growing he would stunt the growth of the tree. So, if you want your investments to grow, then give time, patience and never give up.

Points to Ponder

- Know your goals first. That will tell you the tenure and amount required for the goal. It's more important to have the right amount available at the right time.

- Prioritize your responsibilities.

- Your retirement is your own responsibility and this becomes your goal the day you start earning.

- It's more important to make your kids financially independent by not just providing them Financial support but making sure that they learn about it.

- Quantify the future value of the goal with correct percentage of inflation and considering the right kind of expenses.

- Identify the right kind of asset class based on the tenure of the goal. Once you know where your goal is, it's easier to select a vehicle to reach that goal.

- Take complete advantage of your friend, Power of Compounding.

2.4. Dream Life

This will add quality to your life. These are the things in your life which you will love to do. It will rejuvenate you, give you pleasure and happiness. These are the things you dream of apart from the standard of living. These things will make you feel proud and that's why many people are attracted to it. Things can be like domestic tour, international tour, starting a new business, buying a car, a bigger car, changing a car, bigger house, villa, weekend home, retiring early, pursuing a passion.

There are few things which may come as a part of the standard of living like domestic/international tours or even cars. The point is once you complete or made a provision for Today's enjoyment and proud accomplishments then you can start planning for your Dreamlife.

Dreamlife can be compromised but today's enjoyment and proud accomplishments cannot. If your income is high tours can be a part of your standard of living. There are people who go on tour every year or in a planned way regularly. To allocate funds for your dream life you have to follow the same process of categorization of goals and selection of right asset class.

Many cases its seen that these dreams are postponed till retirement and they never come true. To add flavor in your lives it's important to pursue these dreams along with your responsibilities by forming the right balance. And with the right balance, you can also start pursuing your passion, or hobby which would otherwise have been left behind in the process of completing other responsibilities and liabilities

Once you have allocated the required amount to all your goals, aspirations and retirement fund you can invest the remaining amount for growth with higher risk. You can take 100% exposure in the equity market. Which will help you achieve your dream life if it's a long-term goal?

We suggest that you should use your entire self-created wealth for the first 4 steps of the Pyramid of Financial Success. There is no need to keep something to the next generation in the form of financial assets at the cost of compromising your own life. What you can pass on to the next generation is a good education, good skills to earn money and being a good citizen. You should think of keeping financial assets as a legacy to next-generation only if you have more than your full enjoyment.

Points to Ponder

- Do not live others dream.
- Curate your own dreams.
- Prioritise them.
- Start living your RICH and HAPPY Life.

2.5. Legacy

After planning for first 4 steps of Pyramid of Financial success, if you still have surplus amount with you then this amount can be used to generate a legacy for your next generation. First you have to ensure yourself that you have already completed all your FRM, Today's enjoyment and Proud accomplishment and Dream life.

This legacy would help your next generation to start their life at one step higher socio economy level. They may not have to face the same challenges which you had faced in the process of wealth creation.

Will Creation:

If you want to pass on your wealth to next generation then one of the best ways to do that is by creating a Will. So, if you have wishes about distribution of your wealth after you then you can document it in Will. Will is cost effective as well as tax effective tool. It also facilitates your legal heirs to inherit your estate in a simple and legal way. Registration of will is always not necessary. Unregistered will also has a legal standing. It can be hand written also. Such will be called as holographic will. If there is a chance of dispute in your family after you, we always recommend to have a registered will. Now a days even a video will is accepted legally. If you die without a will (intestate) then your legal heirs may have to do a lot of documentation and hassles to inherit your estate.

There are few points to check while legacy planning, these will help you get a clear picture as to how and what youcan ask yourself while writing a will

1. Who shall manage the execution of your will?

2. Who will look after your Kids?

3. Always keep your will simple

4. Make a list of all that you own

5. Who will inherit what?

6. When should you change or keep updating your Will?

Creating a private trust:

You can also create a private and set the trust deed. It allows you to have control over the trust and freedom to pass on the assets unto the beneficiaries.

Points to Ponder

- You can take higher risk when you reach this step.

- Create a will so that created wealth is passed on as per your wish.

These were the 2 major milestones that we have shared with you as a Master key to Freedom from RRT. If you follow this with discipline you will come out of RRT. To stay out of RRT, continue following it always.

Furthermore, you shall always stay Invested rather than Trapped.

Always remember the Pyramid of Financial Success, and follow all the stages as per given priority.

CHAPTER
Three

A New Beginning - How to Implement all that you have Learned

We saw how and which are the traps, where we get easily trapped in and enter the RRT.

Then we saw the ways of staying away and solution to come out of the RRT.

But the main part starts now. This may be the end of the book but it is a beginning for you. Now is the time to implement what all you could learn and understand from here into your real life.

It's easy to read, listen or tell others how to do and what to do in life. But implementing it is a real challenge. At least in the beginning. But as you cruise through the journey and learn from your own experience and mistakes you will find it getting easier day by day. We are telling this because we have been through it, and now we are financially free, and independent. Successfully achieving our every goal with help of proper planning and the below 4 steps.

3.1. Decide for Freedom from RRT

Until and unless you decide to earn and work for gaining freedom from RRT you won't get it. You need to understand the difference between knowing how to get freedom and doing all that to get freedom.

The first and foremost thing is realization. It is about accepting the fact that you are in a RRT or on the verge of getting into it. The implementation follows later.

This will need a strong mindset. Look around you! All that is seemingly successful today was not the same from day one. The maker of these things had a strong mindset, a positive thought throughout, persistency and consistency which helped them achieve what they wanted.

- Decide what you want

- Stick to that

- Have a positive mindset

3.2. Strategize the path

Once you have decided to earn freedom and come out of RRT forever, next, you need to strategize your plan.

With the help of previous chapters, you can understand your position as of today, and decide where you want to be and accordingly, wisely, use the learned knowledge to strategize your path. Where you want to go, when you want to reach there, how you want to reach there, how much money you shall need there.

Ask these questions for each goal and then prioritize your goals based on which situation shall arrive 1st in your life.

Basically, you can create a map marking your destination, distance, arrival time. and keep that on your pinboard or a place from where you can see it every day, so this shall help you stick to your plan and motivate to achieve your dream on time.

3.3. Execute the Challenging plan

This is a stage where many fail and differentiate men from boys.

If you have decided to earn something, made a plan on how to earn it, then you should be sure and smart to "start earning it". That is implementing or executing the plan.

It's same like food. You know you are hungry and want to eat an omelet. You get all the required things to make an omelet and kept it near the stove hoping it to cook on its own. Highly stupid that would be, right? Of course you will have to cook in order to feed yourself. Same way after knowing and planning how to get freedom you need the execute it.

3.4. Successful freedom from RRT

If you follow the first three steps no one can stop or pull you back in the RRT and earning freedom.

But you need to stay here forever. If you stop following the rules, you might again get trapped.

So to avoid this always keep reviewing your goals, your achievements and places for improvement. You should get a PEST control done on your investment and goals

P- Previewing your investments.

E- Eliminating nonperforming asset class/funds.

S- Switching to performing asset class/funds.

T- Timing your next pest control date.

Our Book

Use this table to know how much amount you need to invest on a monthly basis to fulifil your financial goal.			
Financial Goal Planning			
Value	*Financial Goals*	*Name of the goal*	*How to fill?*
1	Today's Cost	₹ -	Research on this and come with approx. Cost.
2	Inflation (% p.a.)	12.00%	
3	No. years to goal		Age at the time of goal - Today's Age
4	Increased Cost in Future due to Inflation	₹ -	Value#1 * FV factor. For FV factor refer "FV(One Time) Table 2" from Annexure
5	Projected RoR	%	Refer to table "Investment allocation RoR" from Annexure
6	Monthly Investment Required	₹ -	Value#4 * "Monthly Investment Factor"/100 For "Monthly Investment Factor" refer to "Monthly Investment Table 4" from Annexure.

Lets plan for Kids Graduation. There are 2 steps here. First step is to find out the future value of your goal. We use Rate of inflation to calculate the amount required in future when the goal is reached. Second is to find out the monthly amount required to invest.

e.g. Your kids age is 2 years and so he will need an amount after his 12th i.e. at his age of 18. So you have 16 years to build this amount. Today's cost of education that you want to sponsor is 10lac. What would be monthly amount to invest to accumulate the required amount.

	Financial Goal Planning		
Value	**Financial Goals**	**Kids Education**	**How to fill?**
1	Today's Cost	₹ 1,000,000	Your research says that its around Rs 10 Lac.
2	Inflation (% p.a.)	12.00%	
3	No. years to goal	16	Age at the time of goal - Today's Age
4	Increased Cost in Future due to Inflation	₹ 6,130,000	Value#1 * FV factor Value#1 = 10,00,000 FV Factor = 6.13 For FV factor refer "FV(One Time) Table 2" from Annexure
5	Projected RoR	15.00%	Refer to table "Investment allocation RoR" from Annexure
6	Monthly Investment Required	₹ 7,663	Value#4 * "Monthly Investment Factor"/100 Value#4 = 61,30,000 Monthly Investment Factor = 0.125 For "Monthly Investment Factor" refer to "Monthly Investment Table4" from Annexure.

Value#	Retirement	Values	How to fill?
1	Today's Annual Expenses	₹ -	Take it from your current expenses.
2	Inflation (% p.a.)	12.00%	
3	No. years to retire		Age at the time of retirement - Today's Age
4	Annual Expenses in the Year of retirement	₹ -	Value#1 * FV factor. For FV factor refer "FV(One Time) Table 2" from Annexure
5	Years in Retirement		*Life Expentancy - Age of retirement
6	Approx. Retirement fund required	₹ -	Value#4* Value#5 (Assuming Rate of inflation and RoR is same for simplicity purpose)
7	Projected RoR	%	Refer to table "Investment allocation RoR" from Annexure
8	Monthly Investment Required	₹ -	Value#6 * "Monthly Investment Factor" / 100 For "Monthly Investment Factor" refer to "Monthly Investment Table4" from Annexure.

Use this table to know how much amount you need to invest on a monthly basis to retire with enough retirement corpus.

Life Expectancy *			
Life expectancy is expected no. of years that you are going to live. No. of years you are going to live depends on your genes. You may be carrying genes from your maternal And/Or paternal side. So consider the maximum age from the parents/maternal N paternal grand parents age. And taking into consideration medical advancement and facilities available to us you will live longer than them, add 5 to it as precution. Even if you have unhealthy habits or life style it's not life expacancy but the quality of life will affect.			
Value	**Retirement**	**Values**	**How to fill?**
1	Today's Annual Expenses	₹ 360,000	Take it from your current expenses.
2	Inflation (% p.a.)	12.00%	
3	No. years to retire	25	Age at the time of retirement - Today's Age 55 - 30
4	Annual Expenses in the Year of retirement	₹ 6,120,000	Value#1 * FV factor. Value#1= 12,00,000 FV Factor= 17 For FV factor Refered "FV(One Time) Table 2" from Annexure
5	Years in Retirement	35	Life Expectancy=90 Age of retirement=55 *Life Expentancy - Age of retirement
6	Approx. Retirement fund required	₹ 214,200,000	Value#4* Value#5 (Assuming Rate of inflation and RoR is same for simplicity purpose)

7	Projected RoR	15.00%	Refer to table "Investment allocation RoR" from Annexure
8	Monthly Investment Required	₹ 64,260	Value#6 = 21,42,00,000 Monthly Investment Factor = 0.030 (Lookup table for no. of years to retire 25 and Projected RoR 15%) Value#4 * "Monthly Investment Factor" / 100 For "Monthly Investment Factor" refered to "Monthly Investment Table4" from Annexure.

FV (One Time) Table 1

Future value factor- One time investment.

In the following table first column has number of years and 1st row has returns %. Get Future Value factor by matching a value with no. of years and return%.

E.g. If you want to find Future Value factor for 13 years at Returns 10%? follow the row labeled '13' to the right until you find the column that says '10%', the answer is : 3.45.

Years / Rate of Int.	6%	7%	8%	9%	10%	11%	12%	13%	14%	15%	16%	17%
1	1.06	1.07	1.08	1.09	1.10	1.11	1.12	1.13	1.14	1.15	1.16	1.17
2	1.12	1.14	1.17	1.19	1.21	1.23	1.25	1.28	1.30	1.32	1.35	1.37
3	1.19	1.23	1.26	1.30	1.33	1.37	1.40	1.44	1.48	1.52	1.56	1.60
4	1.26	1.31	1.36	1.41	1.46	1.52	1.57	1.63	1.69	1.75	1.81	1.87
5	1.34	1.40	1.47	1.54	1.61	1.69	1.76	1.84	1.93	2.01	2.10	2.19
6	1.42	1.50	1.59	1.68	1.77	1.87	1.97	2.08	2.19	2.31	2.44	2.57
7	1.50	1.61	1.71	1.83	1.95	2.08	2.21	2.35	2.50	2.66	2.83	3.00
8	1.59	1.72	1.85	1.99	2.14	2.30	2.48	2.66	2.85	3.06	3.28	3.51
9	1.69	1.84	2.00	2.17	2.36	2.56	2.77	3.00	3.25	3.52	3.80	4.11
10	1.79	1.97	2.16	2.37	2.59	2.84	3.11	3.39	3.71	4.05	4.41	4.81
11	1.90	2.10	2.33	2.58	2.85	3.15	3.48	3.84	4.23	4.65	5.12	5.62

12	2.01	2.25	2.52	2.81	3.14	3.50	3.90	4.33	4.82	5.35	5.94	6.58
13	2.13	2.41	2.72	3.07	3.45	3.88	4.36	4.90	5.49	6.15	6.89	7.70
14	2.26	2.58	2.94	3.34	3.80	4.31	4.89	5.53	6.26	7.08	7.99	9.01
15	2.40	2.76	3.17	3.64	4.18	4.78	5.47	6.25	7.14	8.14	9.27	10.54
16	2.54	2.95	3.43	3.97	4.59	5.31	6.13	7.07	8.14	9.36	10.75	12.33
17	2.69	3.16	3.70	4.33	5.05	5.90	6.87	7.99	9.28	10.76	12.47	14.43
18	2.85	3.38	4.00	4.72	5.56	6.54	7.69	9.02	10.58	12.38	14.46	16.88
19	3.03	3.62	4.32	5.14	6.12	7.26	8.61	10.20	12.06	14.23	16.78	19.75
20	3.21	3.87	4.66	5.60	6.73	8.06	9.65	11.52	13.74	16.37	19.46	23.11
21	3.40	4.14	5.03	6.11	7.40	8.95	10.80	13.02	15.67	18.82	22.57	27.03
22	3.60	4.43	5.44	6.66	8.14	9.93	12.10	14.71	17.86	21.64	26.19	31.63
23	3.82	4.74	5.87	7.26	8.95	11.03	13.55	16.63	20.36	24.89	30.38	37.01
24	4.05	5.07	6.34	7.91	9.85	12.24	15.18	18.79	23.21	28.63	35.24	43.30
25	4.29	5.43	6.85	8.62	10.83	13.59	17.00	21.23	26.46	32.92	40.87	50.66
26	4.55	5.81	7.40	9.40	11.92	15.08	19.04	23.99	30.17	37.86	47.41	59.27
27	4.82	6.21	7.99	10.25	13.11	16.74	21.32	27.11	34.39	43.54	55.00	69.35
28	5.11	6.65	8.63	11.17	14.42	18.58	23.88	30.63	39.20	50.07	63.80	81.13
29	5.42	7.11	9.32	12.17	15.86	20.62	26.75	34.62	44.69	57.58	74.01	94.93
30	5.74	7.61	10.06	13.27	17.45	22.89	29.96	39.12	50.95	66.21	85.85	111.06
30	5.74	7.61	10.06	13.27	17.45	22.89	29.96	39.12	50.95	66.21	85.85	111.06

Investment Allocation RoR

Goals Tenure	Category of Goal	Asset Class	Debt	Equity	Proected Returns
0 to 3 Months	Ultra-short term	Cash	100%		6.0%
3 months to 3 Yrs.	Short Term	Debt	100%		6.0%
> 3 Yrs to 7 Yrs	Mid Term*	40% Debt + 60% Equity	40%	60%	11.4%
> 7 Yrs to 10 Yrs	Mid Term*	20% Debt + 80% Equity	20%	80%	13.2%
10 Yrs. +	Long Term	Equity		100%	15.0%

Expected RoR	
Equity	15%
Debt	6%

Monthly Investment Table 2

Monthly regular investment for future value Rs.100.

In the following table first column has number of years and 1st row has returns %. Get Monthly investment factor by matching a value with no. of years and return%.

E.g. If you want to find monthly investment factor for Years 10 with Returns @ 13.2%? follow the row labeled '10' to the right until you find the column that says '13.2%', the answer is : 0.401.

Monthly Investment Factor				
Years / Rate of Int.	**6.0%**	**11.4%**	**13.2%**	**15.0%**
1	8.066	7.832	7.756	7.680
2	3.912	3.694	3.624	3.554
3	2.530	2.321	2.254	2.189
4	1.839	1.638	1.575	1.514
5	1.426	1.233	1.173	1.115
6	1.152	0.965	0.908	0.854
7	0.956	0.776	0.722	0.671
8	0.810	0.636	0.585	0.538
9	0.697	0.530	0.482	0.437
10	0.607	0.446	0.401	0.359
11	0.534	0.379	0.336	0.297
12	0.473	0.324	0.284	0.248
13	0.423	0.279	0.241	0.208
14	0.379	0.242	0.206	0.175
15	0.342	0.210	0.176	0.148
16	0.310	0.183	0.152	0.125
17	0.282	0.160	0.131	0.106
18	0.257	0.140	0.113	0.091
19	0.235	0.123	0.098	0.077
20	0.215	0.109	0.085	0.066
21	0.198	0.096	0.074	0.056

22	0.182	0.085	0.064	0.048
23	0.168	0.075	0.056	0.041
24	0.155	0.066	0.049	0.035
25	0.144	0.059	0.042	0.030
26	0.133	0.052	0.037	0.026
27	0.123	0.046	0.032	0.022
28	0.115	0.041	0.028	0.019
29	0.106	0.036	0.025	0.017
30	0.099	0.032	0.022	0.014
31	0.092	0.029	0.019	0.012
32	0.086	0.026	0.017	0.011
33	0.080	0.023	0.014	0.009
34	0.075	0.020	0.013	0.008
35	0.070	0.018	0.011	0.0067
36	0.065	0.016	0.010	0.006
37	0.061	0.014	0.009	0.005
38	0.057	0.013	0.007	0.004
39	0.053	0.011	0.007	0.004
40	0.050	0.010	0.006	0.003

References

//economictimes.indiatimes.com/articleshow/53841350.cms?from=mdr&utm_source=contentofinterest&utm_medium=text&utm_campaign=cppst

https://en.wikipedia.org/wiki/Rat_race

https://en.wikipedia.org/wiki/Inflation_in_India

https://tradingeconomics.com/india/inflation-cpi

https://wiki.mises.org/wiki/Ponzi_scheme

www.ingramcontent.com/pod-product-compliance
Lightning Source LLC
Chambersburg PA
CBHW021939120726
47992CB00001B/53